THE SPELL BOOK FOR NEW WITCHES

the
SPELL
BOOK
for
NEW
WITCHES

ESSENTIAL SPELLS TO
CHANGE YOUR LIFE

Ambrosia Hawthorn

ILLUSTRATIONS BY
Travis Stewart

**ROCKRIDGE
PRESS**

Interior and Cover Designer: Emma Hall
Art Producer: Sue Bischofberger
Editor: Claire Yee
Production Editor: Ashley Polikoff
Illustration © 2019 Travis Stewart

ISBN: Print 978-1-64611-064-3 | eBook 978-1-64611-065-0

R0

TO MY FELLOW WITCHES WHO SEEK OUT MAGIC
TO CREATE CHANGE IN THEIR LIVES.

Contents

Introduction

Welcome to *The Spell Book for New Witches*. I'm Ambrosia, solitary witch and editor of *Witchology Magazine*, a monthly publication for modern witches. I've been a practicing witch for 15 years. I'm here to share my story, knowledge, and craft with you so you can tap into the inner magic and power that's already within you.

That's right—we all have magic within us. But you won't be going to Hogwarts, wiggling your nose to cast spells, or riding a broom. Instead, this book will teach you practical skills, connect you to the natural world, and help you discover the inner witch that has been within you all along. I'll debunk misconceptions about spell-casting and witchcraft and teach you how to create and manifest what you want and need to change your life for the better.

My journey into witchcraft began when I was 13. Young, I know, but the universe works in mysterious ways. My story might be like your story; it might be entirely different. There are many paths to witchcraft, and mine unfolded at the right time for me in my life, just as yours will.

I was pulled into spellcasting for a variety of reasons. I wanted to build my self-confidence at school, earn money for my family, protect myself from bullies, craft love potions for crushes, and bring myself good luck. When I was seven—before I knew anything about witchcraft or spellcasting—I spent every recess and lunch break looking for four-leaf clovers. I knew they were good luck charms and, deep down, that I needed one. After weeks of searching, I finally found one. My mother helped me frame it in a key chain, and I carried it with me everywhere, asking it for luck when I needed it. Looking back, I now realize that key chain was my very first spelled charm. I tell this story to show why spellwork can be so special—spells can come from nearly any source and can be as straightforward or as complex as you'd like.

If you're like me, you're drawn to magic because of the opportunities and changes it enables you to create for yourself. You won't need an eye of newt or the egg of an eagle for the spells contained in this book. All you need is to be present and to have a desire to learn the practice. Wherever you are on your journey, you picked up this book at the right time. Let's dive into the wonderful world of spellcasting and magic.

PART I

PRACTICAL

Magic

There is more to magic than just mixing potions, burning candles, and sewing poppets. Magic is embedded in the world around us, and building a solid foundation rooted in history is vital for a successful spellcaster. In this section, I'll cover crucial practical magic basics: understanding spellcasting and the necessary preparations.

The only thing you need to get started down the path of magic is yourself. Your power is hidden within, waiting to be tapped into, and practicing magic will give you the ability to heal and change yourself and the world.

My hope is that I can help you become the best witch you can be with the essentials contained in these pages. Let's learn what it means to be a practicing witch.

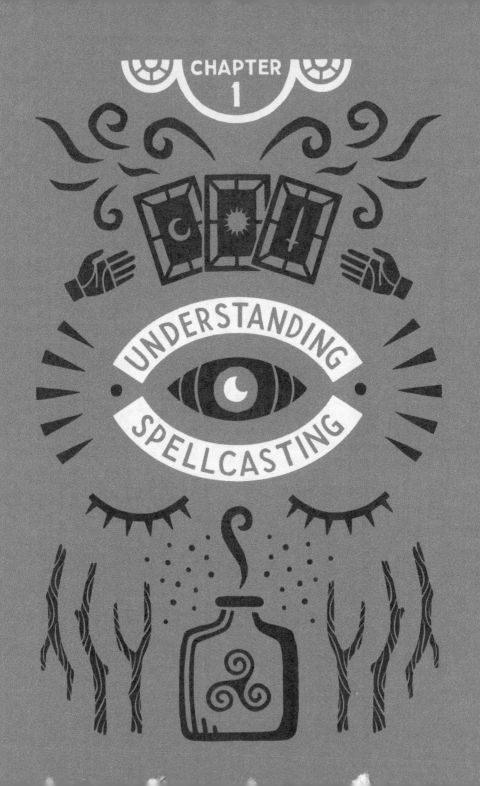

To begin casting spells, we need to cover the who, what, and why of spellcasting. We'll explore terminology, learn the differences between witchcraft and Wicca, and go over common misconceptions, core concepts, and ethics. Once you have these fundamental building blocks, you'll be ready to start creating the changes you want to make in your life.

What Are Spells?

Spells are the practical side of magic. They work by manipulating energy to fulfill a specific intention or purpose. Spells are fueled by emotions, and they work in conjunction with your personal power or the energy in the world around you. To understand what makes a spell effective, we need to first take a look at magic, power, and the nature of energy manipulation.

Magic is the energy that flows through every natural thing. It's neutral energy that is neither good nor evil. Power is the practical art of channeling magic for your use. When you begin bending and channeling magic, you are, in a sense, building up your personal power. It's through this manipulation that you can influence or control the energy around you.

We are all made up of molecules, and the bonds between these molecules contain potential energy. The idea that we can use and channel this energy is not so unusual. In fact, it's easy to recognize when someone is directing their energy toward you. Have you ever "felt" someone's hand hovering a few inches away from your back (even though they weren't actually touching you)? Did you feel a tingling sensation, or even heat? That was the feeling of energy being directed toward you.

Spellcasting is just one of the many ways to manipulate energy. Crystals, stones, herbs, shells, metal, and wood have long been used as energy manipulation tools. And popular mind-body therapies such as tai chi, Reiki, meditation, yoga, acupuncture, and even massage use, raise, and manipulate energy to heal the physical, spiritual, and emotional body. The use of spells isn't as outlandish as one might think!

It's important to note that spells are not get-out-of-jail-free cards. They cannot instantly fix all the problems you may want them to—they take energy, time, effort, focus, and belief to work. It's a common misconception that you can use a spell to make someone fall in love with you or to impose your magic on others. You cannot take away another person's free will with magic.

You must also understand that magic is powerful, and with power comes responsibility. As a spellcaster, your responsibility should be to do no harm and to respect the natural laws. Raising power and casting spells are all temporary manipulations of energy, not permanent ones.

Who Casts Spells?

Anyone who desires to create positive changes in their life can cast a spell. Anyone who is interested enough to pick up this book is already on the right track to begin spellcasting. Spellcasting can help those who seek clarity or purpose on their journey through life. Spells are often cast by Pagans, people who follow a religious or spiritual path based on a respect for nature. Many spellcasters choose a Neo-Pagan path or the tradition of witchcraft, which encompasses modern or hybrid practices such as elemental, secular, hedge, eclectic, or traditional. Each of these categories can be tailored to you to create the perfect path.

ELEMENTAL WITCH

This witch uses the four elements (earth, air, fire, and water) in their practice. They may choose to use all of the elements or only one. Some kinds of witches who heavily use elements in their practice are green, sea, and hearth witches. Green witches build their practice around the element of earth, using herbs, crystals, and wood. Sea witches use the element of water, utilizing the ocean, weather magic, seashells, driftwood, seaweed, and sand. Hearth witches, sometimes called kitchen or cottage witches, use the element of fire to power their cooking, baking, brewing, and crafting of magical items.

SECULAR WITCH (OR NONRELIGIOUS WITCH)

Secular witches do not call upon deities to do their work. They often work with symbolism, metaphors, or archetypes. The secular path is growing in popularity, and many secular witches combine their practice with other types of witchcraft.

HEDGE WITCH

This witch is a little trickier to define. Also known as "hedge riders," these witches cross the boundary into the unknown or into other worlds. Hedge witches often use herbalism to formulate potions, balms, and brews. A hedge witch's practice is often shamanic and Seidh in nature, involving astral projection, lucid dreaming, trance work, and communication with spirits.

ECLECTIC WITCH

Eclectic witches don't fit into any one category. They are often solitary witches who do not belong to a set practice or group. The eclectic witch follows a hodgepodge path of modified traditions that are custom-tailored to their needs and abilities.

TRADITIONAL WITCH

Traditional witches form a larger group with many subgroups, sometimes with ties to Wicca. They often have roots that date back many centuries. In this category, you'll often find ceremony, folk, Hoodoo, hereditary, Celtic, and other Pagan paths. You must be initiated into some of these paths or follow specific rules.

How Spells Relate to Witchcraft and Wicca

By now, you've probably noticed references to Paganism, Wicca, and witchcraft, and you might be wondering what they mean. Wiccans and witches both fall under the umbrella of Paganism, but not all witches are Wiccan, nor are all Wiccans witches. Pagans follow a religious or nonreligious spiritual path that is grounded in respect for nature. Wicca is an earth-centered religion that honors deities, whereas witchcraft is a practice that can encompass a wide variety of paths, religious or not. You can choose a path or make your own.

With all this said, I try not to get too caught up in labeling my practice. Defining your path is not required—in fact, flexibility is what draws so many people to Pagan practices. There is no right or wrong path. I recommend you try a little of everything and build a practice that works for you.

History of Spellcasting

Casting spells has been popular throughout history. The term *spell* originates from the Anglo-Saxon word *spel*, which means "saying" or "story." In ancient civilizations, spells developed alongside language. In ancient Egypt, for example, written stories often contained spells within them.

The term *witch* has been traced to the old Teutonic word *wik*, meaning "to bend." Prior to the fourteenth century, witchcraft and magic enjoyed a golden age. Things changed in 1486 when a now-discredited Catholic clergyman published the *Malleus Maleficarum* (or *Hammer of Witches*), known colloquially as the witch-hunter's handbook. The popularity of the book led to a rise in anti-witchcraft sentiments. In 1542, England's Witchcraft Act made witchcraft and spellcasting punishable by death. In 1692, the Salem witch trials took place in Massachusetts, and 19 people were executed for allegedly practicing witchcraft.

Persecution against witches continued for centuries. The anti-witchcraft movement began to lose steam in the 1900s. In the 1960s and '70s, American society saw an increase in Pagan practices and groups dedicated to Wicca and witchcraft. In 1986, the U.S. Court of Appeals for the Fourth Circuit heard the case *Dettmer v. Landon* and recognized Wicca as an official religion.

Despite the growing acceptance of witchcraft, many witches still fear wrongful persecution. Some prefer to practice their craft in secret—or "in the broom closet."

Core Principles

The core principles of witchcraft relate to how we use energy to manifest change in our environment. Magic is all around us in the form of energy. Practicing spells helps us learn to direct our intentions to manipulate energy. However, your intentions must follow the core principles outlined here.

WORSHIPPING THE ENVIRONMENT AND NATURE

Everything that exists in the natural world is sacred and filled with energy, and the seasons and elements are incorporated in many Pagan rituals and spells. The seasons are to be celebrated and honored. They tell a story of birth, life, death, and rebirth. The elements can be called upon for protection, guidance, and energy.

CELEBRATING FERTILITY AND SEXUALITY

Celebrating life, light, joy, passion, and sensuality ignites the life force within us all. Embracing your fertility and sexuality can be a valuable tool to manifest magic. Many witches celebrate fertility and sexuality during the springtime Pagan sabbats Imbolc, Ostara, and Beltane (covered further in chapter 2 on page 16).

TAPPING INTO INTUITION AND PERSONAL ENERGY

You can influence your environment through your personal energy. Begin with your gut reactions and inklings. Have you ever felt something deep within trying to tell you something—usually a warning? This is your intuition. Once you learn how to channel this energy, you can use it to fuel your spells.

HONORING KARMA AND THE NATURAL BALANCE OF COSMIC LAW

Karma dictates that for every action you put out into the world, you will receive the same action back. The Law of Threefold Return is an old Pagan adage used to caution new witches about the consequences of performing harmful magic: If you cause harm or perform manipulative magic on another, you will receive the same back threefold. Many Pagans live by this karmic force, also known as cosmic law.

KNOWING AND UNDERSTANDING THE AFTERLIFE, SPIRITS, AND REINCARNATION

Many witches believe in an afterlife and view the cycle of birth, life, death, and rebirth as an endlessly turning wheel. Many witches celebrate endings and beginnings during the Pagan sabbat Samhain, when the veil between worlds gets thinner. Samhain is covered in greater depth in chapter 2 on page 16.

The Driving Forces of Spellwork

Spellwork should be driven by a respect for nature and the mystery of the universe. The more you can align yourself with the earth's natural rhythms, the more you can tune in to the mysteries of the world and the more you can learn about the unknown.

MAGIC VS. POWER

Magic is the natural energy that flows through the world, whereas power is the practical art of channeling that energy. Power is within you, waiting to be tapped into, and magic can be found in natural objects.

As a beginner spellcaster, you'll draw mostly from your personal power. However, using only your power can be draining. The spells in this book use items from the natural world, including crystals, herbs, oils, fragrances, wood, and animal items, to lend additional energy.

Another type of power that comes from within you is psychic ability. Some witches have abilities such as precognition, intuition, clairvoyance, psychometry, mediumship, or empathy absorption.

PRECOGNITION is the ability to know things or events before they happen.

INTUITION is the ability to know things without being told.

CLAIRVOYANCE, often referred to as "clear vision," is the ability to reveal what's hidden and is often thought of as "inner sight."

PSYCHOMETRY is the ability to read the energy of an object or sense the details about the person who once had the object.

MEDIUMS receive messages from the spirit world and can also channel spirits.

EMPATHS can sense the feelings and emotions of others while often absorbing energies from others.

"GOOD MAGIC" VS. "BAD MAGIC"

The non-magical community often labels magic as "good" or "bad." In the magical community, however, there isn't a distinction between "good" or "bad" magic. Magic isn't black and white—its effects depend on the energy of the spellcaster's intentions.

Using magic for harm, to get revenge, to alter someone else's free will, or to curse someone are all examples of what some might call "black magic" or unethical practice. Using magic to heal, empower, or uplift is often called "white magic." Many witches add "white witch" to their titles to avoid the common misconception that all witches are evil or bad.

You might be tempted to use ill will in your magic if you are confronted with a curse, bad rumors, a malevolent spirit, or a stalker. If you do, however, you may open yourself up to the consequences of karma or cosmic law, discussed earlier on page 13. Ethics in magic are the same as ethics in any other area of life, and in the end, you'll be held personally responsible for your actions.

CHAPTER
2

PREPARING
TO CAST A

SPELL

Before you dive into spellwork, you must learn how to be a successful spellcaster. Learning the foundations of spellcasting will help you build and sustain a rewarding practice. These basics include how to perform a spell, where to practice, what tools to use, and how to access your power. You'll also learn about common symbols and important dates, seasons, and cycles.

How to Perform a Spell

When you perform a spell, you either create new energy or manipulate existing energy. The basic elements of a spell are crafting and casting. "Crafting" refers to choosing a location for your spell, clearing away unwanted energies, casting a circle of protection, raising energy, and setting your intentions. "Casting" refers to performing the spellwork, closing the circle of protection, and observing the results. The specific steps of crafting and casting vary among traditions.

When you craft, you must first dedicate a location for your spell and clear the area of unwanted old or negative energies. Many witches create a permanent altar or designate a sacred space specifically for their spellwork.

Next, you must cast a circle of protection to protect yourself from unwanted attention or outside influences. There are many methods to casting a circle. In traditional witchcraft, one might call upon a god or goddess, and a secular witch would likely call upon a significant object infused with natural energy or create a wall of their own energy (significant objects are discussed further on page 28).

Once you're inside your circle of protection, you'll draw from one or more energy sources to fuel your spell. This energy might come from a god or goddess, from a natural object like a crystal or talisman, or from yourself.

After your spell is complete, you must withdraw the energy from the spell to close your circle of protection. How you close the circle should mirror the method you used to cast it in the first place.

Where to Practice Spellwork

Witches practice spellwork in all sorts of places. You may dedicate a single room as your sacred space, or you may use many different locations unique to specific spells. If you are in the broom closet, your room might be your only option, and that's perfectly okay.

Lots of spellwork can be done indoors. You can do most spells for potions, teas, and baking in your kitchen, whereas you'll probably do bath spells in your bathroom. You'll probably practice outdoors for spellwork that uses the moon, astrology, seasons, nature, or the weather. Try to find a peaceful and private outdoor space where you won't be distracted or interrupted (if you have one, a backyard is ideal for this).

Regardless of where you do your spellwork, safety should be your first priority. When working with fire magic in any location, for example, it's important to always use fire-safe tools and have a fire extinguisher nearby. Above all, you should practice your craft somewhere that makes you feel comfortable and safe.

How to Create an Altar

An altar is a platform or table that serves as a work space for spells, ceremonies, rituals, meditations, and other magical practices. You can tailor your altar to match a specific spell or complement a month or season. For example, many witches create themed altars for the eight Pagan sabbats (covered further on page 22). If you're outdoors, you can use a stump or flat rock as an altar. If you travel frequently, make a portable altar kit to carry with you.

The tools on your altar will differ depending on the traditions you follow. An altar can be created on any budget—as long as it's functional, it can be as simple or complex as you'd like. Many witches use a north-facing altar filled with items or tools that represent each of the four elements (earth, air, fire, and water). You can include any other items you want, such as a book of shadows, crystals, seasonal items, or other offerings. You may need to adjust your altar for different spells. Preparing your altar should be fun, so feel free to let your creativity flourish.

How to Access Your Powers

Before you can practice magic, you must learn to access your personal power. Do this by clearing your mind and banishing distractions to achieve a relaxed, focused mental state. Many witches meditate for five to ten minutes at the beginning of their practice. Try incorporating music, candles, incense, essential oils, or guided meditations.

Once you have cleared your mind, you must center, raise, and ground your energy. The first step, centering, is the initial process of visualizing your energy in order to access it. When you center your energy, you should be able to feel it expand and contract. Focus on connecting with your body's energy and try to feel a sense of balance and equilibrium.

Next, you must raise your energy. Beginner witches sometimes use too much of their own energy during this step and end up draining themselves. You can prevent this from happening in your spellwork by using items like crystals, stones, or full moon–charged water for extra energy. These items have energy of their own that you can combine with your energy to raise enough power to cast a spell. To use an energy-charged item in a spell, hold the item—for example, a crystal—in your hand. Visualize the energy in your hand mixing with the crystal's energy. Feeling heat in your hand at this point is normal—it means that you have harnessed energy and are ready to use it in a spell.

When you have completed the spell, ground your energy to rebalance your energy levels. Grounding releases excess energy left over after you cast a spell. If you're new to spellcasting, I recommend getting some grounding crystals or stones, such as hematite, moonstone, obsidian, and sodalite. To begin grounding, you'll want to get as physically close to the ground as you can. Proximity to the ground will help foster an easier and smoother connection. Now visualize all the excess energy leaving your body while also focusing on your breathing. On every exhale, release a little bit more energy, feeling it flow to the ground.

Community Spellwork vs. Solitary Spellwork

Now that you've learned about the basics of spellcasting, it's time to cover one of the most common beginner witch questions: Do you need to be in a coven to practice magic or cast spells? The answer is no. Being in a coven is a choice—one that only you can make.

COVENS

A coven is a group of witches in a community who practice and perform spells, rituals, and ceremonies together. The term *coven—* from the Latin word *convenire*, meaning "to come together"—was popularized by Margaret Murray in her 1921 book *The Witch-Cult in Western Europe*. In a coven, there are usually one or two leaders, known as either a High Priest or High Priestess. When you cast spells within a coven, you're often sharing the workload and being given a step or task of a larger spell. The spells contained in this book are written for the solitary spellcaster, but they can also be used in group practice.

Covens aren't as prominent today as they once were. Some covens earned a reputation for controversy and corruption, and a few are said to have concealed underlying issues like toxic power dynamics, sexual exploitation, coerced nudity, bribery, and other inappropriate activities. As a result of the troubled history of covens, many witches today prefer solitary practice.

If you have a solitary practice, you cast spells primarily on your own, but you can still join a community of other witches, Wiccans, or Pagans. Many witches nowadays come together in a "circle," which is an open gathering that doesn't have the structure of a coven. Often, witches gather in circles to honor the full moon, complete a ritual, or discuss spirituality and other topics. Circles allow witches with different practices to work together. Finding the right group of witches for you takes a bit of research and time. Visit meetings, meet other members, and ask questions. Most importantly, if you ever feel pressured or in danger, remember you have every right to exit the situation.

Calendars, Seasons, and Cycles

Using the calendars, seasons, and cycles is an effective way to connect with nature and the magic around you. The important days to remember include the solstices, equinoxes, and sabbats that make up the Wheel of the Year.

THE FOUR SEASONS AND EQUINOXES

The four seasons are marked by the four solar festivals: the spring equinox, the summer solstice, the fall equinox, and the winter solstice. There is also a festival in the middle of each season, and these four dates are known as halfway celebrations. Together, the solar festivals and halfway celebrations make up the eight Pagan sabbats: Samhain, Yule, Imbolc, Ostara, Beltane, Litha, Lughnasadh, and Mabon. A sabbat is a celebration to honor the changing of seasons. *Sabbat* comes from the Latin word *sabbatum*, meaning "day of rest."

SAMHAIN (*sow-in* or *sah-win*)—This sabbat represents the last harvest, the end of summer, and the beginning of the witch's New Year. Samhain is usually celebrated on October 31 in the northern hemisphere and April 30 in the southern hemisphere. Samhain occurs when the veil between worlds is at its thinnest, allowing the dead and the fae (nature spirits, like fairies, elves, and goblins) to enter our realm. It also coincides with Halloween. On Samhain, honor spirits, contact your ancestors, or celebrate life and death.

YULE (*yool* or *ewe-elle*)—Celebrated from December 21 to 22 in the northern hemisphere and from June 21 to 22 in the southern hemisphere. Yule is the winter solstice—the longest night of the year. After Yule, the nights get shorter as springtime approaches. Yule represents the promise of light and the rebirth of the sun. Use this time to honor the transformative energies of life and death and celebrate with family and friends.

IMBOLC (*im-bullg*)—Celebrated on February 1 in the northern hemisphere and August 1 in the southern hemisphere. Often called Candlemas or Brigid's Day, Imbolc marks a time when life starts to reappear after the slumber and darkness of winter. Use this time to celebrate fertility, love, and creativity.

OSTARA (*oh-star-ah*)—Celebrated from March 20 to 21 in the northern hemisphere and from September 20 to 21 in the southern hemisphere. Ostara is the spring equinox—one of two days all year when daytime and nighttime are exactly the same length. After Ostara, the days get longer as summer approaches. Ostara celebrates renewal, balance, and rebirth—use this time to honor new life and new ideas.

BELTANE (*bel-tyn* or *bey-al-tin-ah*)—Celebrated on May 1 in the northern hemisphere and November 1 in the southern hemisphere. Often called May Day, Beltane celebrates life, new beginnings, passion, and romance. Use this time to honor unions and springtime energies.

LITHA (*lie-tha* or *lee-tha*)—Celebrated from June 21 to 22 in the northern hemisphere and from December 21 to 22 in the southern hemisphere. Litha is the summer solstice—the longest day of the year. Use this time to honor the sun, vitality, growth, and empowerment.

LUGHNASADH (*loo-nah-sah*)— Celebrated on August 1 in the northern hemisphere and February 1 in the southern hemisphere. Often called Lammas, Lughnasadh is the first harvest festival, a time to reap the seeds sowed all year in preparation for the colder months to come. Use this time to celebrate gratitude, abundance, and creativity.

MABON (*may-bun*)—Celebrated from September 22 to 23 in the northern hemisphere and from March 20 to 21 in the southern hemisphere. Mabon is the fall equinox—the only other day of the year when daytime and nighttime are exactly the same length. After Mabon, the days get shorter as winter approaches. Mabon is also the second harvest festival of the year, a time to celebrate with loved ones and give thanks (it is also nicknamed "witches' Thanksgiving").

MOON CYCLES

The moon plays an important role in spellcasting. It orbits Earth every 29 and a half days, completing the lunar cycle. During the lunar cycle, the moon waxes from new to full and then wanes back to new, at which time a new cycle begins. In the next section, we'll discuss the moon's phases and how to use them in your practice.

The Role of the Moon

The moon's energy changes throughout the lunar cycle. As such, it's important to know which phase the moon is in when casting a spell.

The lunar cycle begins with the **new moon**. The new moon offers limitless potential and a clean slate. This is the perfect phase for casting spells relating to new beginnings, personal improvement, manifestation, peace, and divination.

The **waxing moon**, or first quarter moon, marks the halfway point between a new moon and a full moon. During this phase, the moon's energy is growing. As such, this phase is ideal for spells that also need energy to grow, such as those relating to your creativity, luck, courage, health, finances, balance, motivation, and love.

The **full moon** occurs when the moon is round and at full brightness in the sky. The moon's energy is strongest when it is full, and you should take advantage of this time to charge your tools for upcoming spellwork. During this phase, some witches perform an Esbat, or a full moon ritual. The full moon phase is perfect for spells relating to spirituality, decisions, health, and success.

The **waning moon**, or last quarter moon, marks the moon's descent back to a new moon. During this phase, perform spells relating to grounding, release, eliminating, banishing, transitions, obstacles, and balance.

Just before the new moon, there's a **dark moon**, or balsamic moon. During this phase, the moon is shrouded in darkness and is not visible in the night sky. The dark moon phase is ideal for spells relating to intuition, banishing, protection, cleansing, meditation, and energy work.

FULL MOON

Every month of the year has a full moon, and each of these full moons is different. There are only twelve months in the year, but there are thirteen full moons per year. This results in a "blue moon," which is a second full moon that can appear in any of the months. Below is a list of what each month's moon represents.

JANUARY MOON—the wolf, cold, or birch moon; emphasis on energies of protection, intuition, and wisdom

FEBRUARY MOON—the quickening, snow, hunger, chaste, or rowan moon; energies of purification, growth, and healing

MARCH MOON—the storm, worm, seed, sap, or ash moon; energies of rebirth and awakening

APRIL MOON—the hare, wind, grass, pink, or alder moon; ideal for spells relating to change, balance, emotions, and planning

MAY MOON—the flower, merry, milk, planting, or willow moon; ideal for spells relating to building energy, intuition, and connections

JUNE MOON—the rose, mead, strawberry, strong sun, or hawthorn moon; excellent for protection, strengthening, preventive, and maintaining spells

JULY MOON—the wort, hay, thunder, blessing, buck, or oak moon; perfect for spells relating to divination, dreamwork, and psychic abilities

AUGUST MOON—the corn, red, sturgeon, or holly moon; used for spells relating to rebirth, abundance, prosperity, and renewal

SEPTEMBER MOON—the harvest or hazel moon; ideal for spells relating to lightness and darkness, emotions, and mental and physical well-being

OCTOBER MOON—the blood, hunter's, or vine moon; perfect for spells relating to letting go, cleansing, karma, growth, divination, dreamwork, and spirits

NOVEMBER MOON—the mourning, frost, beaver, or ivy moon; helpful for spells relating to shedding habits or relationships, fresh starts, and connections

DECEMBER MOON—the long nights, cold, or reed moon; ideal for spells relating to endurance, rebirth, and transformation

BLUE MOON—stronger in energy than other moons

Tools and Clothing

Every spellcaster needs tools to do their work—but having a big collection of expensive tools or fancy jewelry won't enhance your power on its own. First, you have to learn the foundations. In this section, we'll go over some of the basics.

SPELLCASTING CLOTHES

What someone wears to practice magic varies depending on the tradition they follow. Members of a coven or circle sometimes wear robes. In some Wicca traditions, practicing naked is the norm. You should put thought into what you wear to cast spells, but you don't need anything elaborate or expensive—mainly, you need to feel comfortable while sitting, standing, moving, and sometimes dancing. Wearing jewelry, crystals, or talismans can also enhance your energy.

SIGNIFICANT OBJECTS

Witches use a variety of tools and significant objects to enhance their craft. The tools I can't live without are my book of shadows, altar bowl, mortar and pestle, candles, crystals, incense, divination tools, besom, and wand. Some of the spells in this book use other significant objects like pendants, jewelry, and poppets. Here are some of the most commonly used tools and objects.

Book of Shadows

Many witches use a book of shadows, or a grimoire, to keep a record of their practice. A witch's book of shadows might include spells, meditations, rituals, recipes, and miscellaneous notes.

Altar Bowl

Finding a good altar bowl is a little harder than it might sound. Your bowl must be able to hold salt, herbs, crystals, and water (for potions or for scrying). I use a black or natural bowl that is wide and fairly deep.

Mortar and Pestle

Grinding your own herbs by hand can help you set an intention in your spell-work. I use a mortar and pestle to grind herbal mixtures for spell bottles, charm bags and pouches, incense, candle dressings, and poppets.

Candles

The spells in this book use a variety of candles. Large pillar or taper candles are perfect for long-term spells, whereas tea lights or votive candles are ideal for single-use spells. Burn times vary, but on average, 5- to 7-inch pillar candles will burn for 90 to 100 hours, smaller votive candles will burn for 10 to 15 hours, 12-inch taper candles will burn for 9 to 12 hours, and tea lights will

burn for just 4 to 6 hours. Be sure to keep your lit candles away from combustible material, flammable liquids, and gases.

Crystals

Crystals are crucial tools in spellcasting. I like to think of crystals as batteries of energy that can be recharged. The spells in this book use a variety of crystals and stones, but I recommend starting out with a clear quartz crystal, since it can be used in place of other crystals in almost

every spell. You must cleanse your crystals of old energies between uses. A list of common crystals is on page 33.

Incense

Incense is often used in spellwork to aid in cleansing, purifying, and setting intentions. Incense can be combustible or noncombustible. Combustible incense contains saltpeter to help it burn and comes in the form of store-bought cones, sticks, and coils. Noncombustible incense must be burned  on a charcoal disc on a heat-proof dish. It usually comes in the form of loose incense mix or smudge sticks (bundles of dried herbs bound with string).

Divination Tools

Different witches use different tools to help them "divine," or foresee, the future. I always keep a deck of tarot cards on my altar (I recommend the Rider-Waite deck). I also always have a bag of runestones on hand. Runestones are stones inscribed with the  Runic alphabet—a pre-Latin alphabet with Germanic origins. I use the Elder Futhark Runic alphabet, which contains 24 letters.

Besom

A besom, or witch broom, is used to sweep an altar space or room. It clears away old energies from previous spellwork or rituals. Many witches use a miniature besom to clean their altar, tools, and ingredients.

Poppet

A poppet is a handmade (often hand-sewn) doll that represents a person in spellwork. You can make poppets with any fabric, but if you're a beginner sewer, I recommend working with felt and sewing with a large embroidery needle and embroidery thread.

Wand or Athame

A wand is used to direct energy in spellwork. Wands are often used in place of the traditional athame (witch's knife) or planchette (pointer). Wands can be made from various types of wood and sometimes have crystals or stones attached to them.

A Sample Witch's Pantry

Many of the spells in this book use ingredients that you can find at your local grocery store! Below is a list of some commonly used ingredients. Less common ingredients can be purchased at a witchcraft specialty supply store or ordered online.

ESSENTIAL OILS are concentrated oils that carry the fragrance of the plant they are made from. They are potent, so most spells use them in sparing quantities. Make sure you dilute the essential oils with water or a carrier oil before placing them on your skin. The essential oils used most frequently in this book are:

- Bergamot
- Cedar
- Eucalyptus
- Geranium
- Jasmine
- Lavender
- Patchouli
- Peppermint
- Rose
- Rosemary
- Sage
- Sandalwood

CARRIER OILS are base oils (usually plant or vegetable based) that are used to dilute essential oils. They are usually affordable, and you can find most at a grocery store. Frequently used carrier oils include:

- Almond oil
- Avocado oil
- Coconut oil
- Jojoba oil
- Olive oil
- Rosehip oil

HERBS, SPICES, FLOWERS, AND CRYSTALS make up crucial ingredients in many of the spells in this book. Frequently used herbs, spices, flowers, and crystals include:

HERBS (FRESH AND DRIED)

- Basil
- Bay leaf (dried)
- Lemon balm
- Mint
- Mugwort
- Orange zest (fresh)
- Rosemary
- St. John's wort
- Thyme

SPICES

- Allspice
- Black pepper
- Black salt
- Cardamom
- Cayenne pepper
- Cinnamon (ground and sticks)
- Cloves (whole and ground)
- Crushed chili flakes
- Cumin
- Epsom salt
- Ginger (fresh and dried)
- Nutmeg
- Sage
- Sea salt
- Star anise

FLOWERS (ALL DRIED UNLESS OTHERWISE SPECIFIED)

- Chamomile
- Geranium petals
- Hibiscus flowers
- Jasmine
- Lavender
- Marigold flowers
- Rose hips
- Rose petals (fresh and dried)
- Violet flowers
- Yarrow flowers

CRYSTALS

- Aventurine
- Bloodstone
- Carnelian
- Citrine
- Clear quartz
- Emerald
- Garnet
- Hematite
- Lapis lazuli
- Obsidian
- Peridot
- Pyrite
- Rose quartz
- Selenite
- Smoky quartz
- Sodalite
- Tigereye
- Turquoise

Signifiers

Spellwork frequently uses symbols and signifiers. Although many of the same symbols are used across witchcraft traditions, compiling a comprehensive list of symbols would be an impossible task. Here are some of the most frequently used symbols and signifiers.

SYMBOLS

Symbols allow you to communicate and cast spells in shorthand. The most important symbols to learn are the pentacle, elemental triangles, circles, moon phases, sigils, and knots.

PENTACLE—A five-pointed star, or pentagram, within a circle. The pentacle has become a defining symbol of modern Paganism, and you'll often see it inscribed on tools. It has close associations with the elements, altars, sacred circles, protection, divine power, and spirituality.

ELEMENTAL TRIANGLES—These are four different triangles that represent the elements of the natural world (earth, air, water, and fire). You can use the elemental triangles in place of an element when you don't have direct access to it.

CIRCLES—This shape represents sacred space and protective energy. Circles are also associated with wholeness, ongoing energy, spirit, and the astrological symbols of the sun and moon.

MOON PHASES—Each phase of the lunar cycle (new, waxing, full, waning, and dark) has a corresponding symbol. Knowing the differences between the moon's phases—discussed earlier in this chapter on page 25—will help you in your spellwork and make it easier to read calendars and track astrological movements.

SIGILS—These are unique symbols that you create to hold a specific intention or meaning. They can be carved, drawn, or sewn into an object to embody energy. This spell book will teach you how to make several kinds of custom sigils to aid your practice.

KNOTS—Knots in spellwork frequently symbolize connection, protection, and binding.

COLORS

Different colors hold different meanings in witchcraft. Many of the spells in this book use certain colors to fulfill specific intentions. Here is a list of colors and their associations.

WHITE—cleansing, protection, truth, purity, healing, and clear vision

BLACK—negativity, reversal, banishing, protection, forgiveness, grief, and leaving a relationship

BROWN—uncertainty, grounding, protection, ideas, and locating lost objects

GRAY—neutrality, settling emotions, invisibility, and compromises

RED—love, passion, strength, courage, pleasure, action, and determination

ORANGE—fertility, creativity, self-esteem, confidence, abundance, and energy

YELLOW—confidence, wisdom, happiness, memory, concentration, logic, and mental exercises

GREEN—money, luck, fertility, healing, growth, and prosperity

BLUE—health, calming, confidence, truth, success, protection, and depression

PURPLE—power, psychic abilities, divination, psychic protection, dreams, and memory

PINK—love, honor, romance, friendship, affection, trust, and attraction

GOLD—worldly achievement, wealth, and recognition

SILVER—divination, goals, awakening psychic abilities, and visions

SONGS AND CHANTS

Words, chants, songs, and incantations are used to raise a spell's energy, power, and intention. You can also write your own chants or incantations.

Before You Begin Your Spellwork

Before we begin casting spells, it's important to learn about karma, intention, reincarnation, and free will. These topics will elevate your foundation and allow you to make educated decisions and be mindful of the consequences of your spellwork.

KARMA AND INTENTION

We already covered the basics of karma on page 13, but you must also be mindful of your intentions and how they intersect with karma. You must practice personal responsibility when setting intentions for your spells—remember that the intentions you set out into the world will eventually make their way back to you.

REINCARNATION

Many witches and Wiccans believe in spirits, an afterlife, and reincarnation, and this is where karma may pay you a visit. If you have
lots of bad luck or negative life experiences, it is thought to be the
result of bad deeds in past lives.

FREE WILL

As a witch, you hold the power to manifest change, but no matter
what, you must respect free will. Trying to alter another person's
free will can have grave consequences. Be careful when casting
spells that include others and be mindful of your intentions.

frequent Instructions in Spells

The spells in this book include many of the same basic instructions. Before we dive into specific spells, here are some common instructions you'll find and what they mean.

CLEANSING YOUR ALTAR OR AREA OF SPELLWORK. This is the first step of nearly every spell in this book, and it refers to physically cleaning your space as well as clearing away old energies. You can use your own energy, a besom, incense, or crystals to cleanse your space. When you cleanse your space, you can also consecrate it, or dedicate it for your spellwork.

PURIFYING YOUR TOOLS AND INGREDIENTS. Before you begin most spells, you'll need to purify the tools and ingredients. There are a few ways to purify an object: You can pass it through incense smoke, wave a besom over it, or wash it with water. There are a few practical rules of thumb. For instance, don't use water to purify items that could be damaged by getting wet, such as metal jewelry, wood, and some crystals, and don't use incense smoke to purify objects if you're in an area with poor ventilation. These spells won't specify how to purify objects unless the spell requires something very specific—generally, you can use your judgment.

CHARGING WATER. Several spells in part 2 call for water charged under a full moon. To charge a bowl of water, simply leave it out overnight beneath a full moon. This allows the moon's lunar energy to transmit into the water and energize it.

CHARGING (OR RECHARGING) A CRYSTAL. You can charge a crystal by placing it under the light of the full moon. If you don't have time to wait for a full moon, you can hold the crystal in your hand to charge it with your own energy. But beware using too much of your own energy!

RECHARGING A FINISHED ITEM. In order to recharge an item that you created in a spell, perform the same spell on it again. For example, if a spell directed you to make a spelled pendant, you could recharge the pendant by performing the spell on it a second time. Recharging items helps them retain their magical properties.

ANOINTING AN ITEM. To anoint something is to rub it with oil.

SCRYING, WATER SCRYING, FIRE SCRYING, OR GAZING. Scrying is the process of looking into a substance and using it to see the future. In the spells in this book, you'll usually be looking into a fire, the flame of a candle, a bowl of water, smoke from incense, or a crystal sphere.

USING YOUR WAND. A wand will help you direct and focus your energy. To use, hold your wand firmly and treat it as an extension of your hand. Use it to direct and channel your energy while making intentions, creating energy barriers, or activating crystal grids.

IMBUING ITEMS WITH YOUR INTENTION. To imbue an item with your intention, hold it within your hands, close your eyes, and visualize your desire. This will allow some of your energy to transfer into the item. Your intentions, energy, and desires will manifest outcomes for your spells.

PART II

THE Spells

When we cast spells, we are usually looking to create change in our lives. But we must learn to be hyperaware of the energy and intentions we put into our spells. New spellcasters are often tempted to cast spells with ill intentions or practice witchcraft when their emotions are heightened or unstable—but doing so can lead to grave consequences.

When you find your emotions are spiraling out of control, focus your energy on a self-love spell (page 45) to get your feelings in check. This will help you regain a sense of calm, and no one else will get harmed in the process.

Finally, always approach spellcasting in a thoughtful, reasonable, and careful way. Remember, it's up to you to choose how you will use the power of your intentions.

Attracting or finding love is popular in spellcasting. It can also be dangerous, because if you aren't mindful, you may inadvertently violate cosmic law. Make informed decisions about what's right and wrong as you perform these spells. The spells in this section will allow you to attract, increase, find, get over, and inspire love in your life.

Rose Attraction Potion

This potion is ideal for attracting potential new suitors or admirers into your life. It involves easy-to-find herbs and tools that you likely already have in your home. A rose is the best flower to use in this recipe due to its association with love.

WHEN TO PERFORM THIS SPELL:
On a Friday or during a
   waxing moon

TIME TO ALLOT FOR THE SPELL:
15 minutes

WHERE TO PERFORM THE SPELL:
Kitchen

INGREDIENTS/TOOLS:
Small pot
1 cup water
1 teaspoon dried rose petals
1 teaspoon dried
   hibiscus flowers
1 teaspoon dried
   lavender flowers
Pinch of cinnamon
Muslin cloth or strainer
Cup for drinking

1. Cleanse your kitchen.

2. In a small pot, boil the water as you set your intentions.

3. Remove the pot from the heat. Place the rose petals, hibiscus, lavender, and cinnamon one at a time into the pot. As you do this, repeat the words *"Infuse, imbue, impart, immerse"* four times.

4. Slowly stir the mixture as you visualize the energy of attraction wrapping around the herbs in the pot. Allow the potion to steep for 10 minutes.

5. Strain the potion into a cup and drink.

Self-Love Bath

Bath magic is ideal for cleansing away old energy and for allowing new, nurturing energy to take root. This spell is perfect for generating more self-love for your physical, mental, emotional, psychological, and spiritual self.

WHEN TO PERFORM THIS SPELL:
On a Monday, Friday, or during a full moon

TIME TO ALLOT FOR THE SPELL:
30 minutes

WHERE TO PERFORM THE SPELL:
Bathroom

INGREDIENTS/TOOLS:
1 cup Epsom salt
3 drops jasmine essential oil
3 drops rose essential oil
Lighter or matches
Pink pillar candle
Rose quartz crystal

1. Cleanse your bathroom.

2. Fill your bathtub with warm or hot water.

3. Add the Epsom salt and jasmine and rose essential oils.

4. As the tub fills, light the candle and set it in a safe location nearby.

5. Hold the rose quartz in your dominant hand and soak in the bath for 20 minutes. Focus on the things you love about yourself. Feel the bathwater infuse your body and the rose quartz with love and healing energies.

6. After 20 minutes, drain the bath and blow out the candle.

7. Whenever you need a boost of self-love, light the candle and hold the rose quartz.

Getting Over Love Spell

This spell will help you move on from past love. The ideal time to cast this spell is after a full moon, once the moon begins to wane back into the darkness of the new moon.

WHEN TO PERFORM THIS SPELL:
During a waning moon

TIME TO ALLOT FOR THE SPELL:
15 minutes

WHERE TO PERFORM THE SPELL:
Altar

INGREDIENTS/TOOLS:
3 drops clove essential oil
1 tablespoon olive oil
Small dish
Black pillar candle
Lighter or matches
Pen and paper
Large bowl
Small bowl
About ½ cup water

1. Cleanse your altar.

2. Mix the clove essential oil and olive oil in a small dish. Using your fingers, anoint your black candle. Be careful not to get oil on the wick.

3. Light the candle and focus on your intentions to cut ties with your ex-lover.

4. Write a goodbye message to the feelings that no longer serve you. Put the message in a large bowl.

5. Fill a small bowl with water and place your hands into it, cleansing away pain, anger, and resentment.

6. Lift some water out of the bowl with your hands and throw it on the paper, enforcing your goodbye.

7. Squeeze the paper and discard it, removing it from your life.

8. Whenever you feel old feelings returning, light your anointed candle.

Custom Love Sigil

Creating a custom love sigil is fun and creative! This sigil is perfect for drawing more attention to you from your love interest. It's also the perfect way to illuminate your true feelings.

WHEN TO PERFORM THIS SPELL:
On a Friday or during a
  new moon

TIME TO ALLOT FOR THE SPELL:
10 minutes

WHERE TO PERFORM THE SPELL:
Altar

INGREDIENTS/TOOLS:
2 sheets of paper
Pen with red ink

1. Cleanse your altar.

2. Write your name and your love interest's name on one of the sheets of paper with a red pen.

3. Deconstruct the letters of the names into their basic strokes, like curves, dots, dashes, and lines. Draw these strokes below the names on the same paper.

4. Still on the same sheet of paper, combine the strokes to form the outline of a shape. This could be a square, a heart, a cross, or a triangle. Place any remaining circles, arcs, and dashes along the lines or around the shape. This shape is your love sigil.

5. Redraw your love sigil, now coded with your intentions, on the second sheet of paper. Carry it with you.

Restore Love Knot Spell

Did you have an argument that with your loved one that you regret? Do you want to bring your romance back to the beginning? This spell is perfect for returning the energy of your relationship back to how it was when the love was pure and new.

WHEN TO PERFORM THIS SPELL:
On a Monday or during a new moon

TIME TO ALLOT FOR THE SPELL:
45 to 60 minutes

WHERE TO PERFORM THE SPELL:
Altar

INGREDIENTS/TOOLS:
Desire Incense (page 57) or Positivity Incense (page 202)
Charcoal disc and heat-proof dish (optional)
3 red tea light candles
Lighter or matches
2 (12-inch) pieces of string in different colors

1. Cleanse your altar.

2. Burn your Desire or Positivity Incense. If your incense is loose, burn it on a charcoal disc on a heat-proof dish. Set up the candles in a triangular configuration.

3. Light the candles and focus on your intention of restoring love.

4. Hold the two strings together and tie a simple overhand knot at one end. As you do this, say, *"Knot of love, revive what has vanished."*

5. Tie another knot and say, *"Knot of passion, bring back the delight."*

6. Tie a third knot and say, *"Knot of adoration, renew what was damaged."*

7. Tie a fourth and final knot and say, *"Knot of desire, mend and rewrite."*

8. Allow the candles to burn while you meditate, visualizing the love you want restored. Continue until 45 to 60 minutes have passed.

Burning Heartbreak Spell

Burn away heartbreak using the element of fire. This spell uses photographs and lemon balm, which is known for its healing properties. It will help you recover from the emotional pain of a broken relationship.

WHEN TO PERFORM THIS SPELL:
On a Monday or during a
dark moon

TIME TO ALLOT FOR THE SPELL:
30 to 45 minutes

WHERE TO PERFORM THE SPELL:
Altar or outdoor firepit

INGREDIENTS/TOOLS:
Outdoor firepit, if outside
Fire-safe bowl, if indoors at
your altar
Lighter or matches
2 photographs, one of you and
another of the person who
broke your heart
Small handful dried lemon balm
Sea salt (optional)

1. Cleanse your altar or outdoor firepit area.

2. If performing the spell indoors, use a lighter to ignite the edge of each photo before placing it inside your fire-safe bowl. If spellcasting outside, you may toss each photo one at a time into the fire. As the photographs burn, say,
   "With this photo, I ease my sorrow;
   with this fire, I burn away this grief;
   with these ashes, I take away this pain."

3. When you have burned both of your photos, toss the lemon balm into the fire or into the bowl.

4. Optional: Collect some of the ash from the fire and mix it with sea salt to create a powerful nonedible black salt that can be sprinkled or thrown around you to banish negative emotions in the future.

Mending Heartbreak Talisman

This spell will teach you how to create a talisman that will assist your heart's healing. Your talisman must be worn at all times. This recipe uses cayenne pepper, which provides support during separations and emotional heartache.

WHEN TO PERFORM THIS SPELL:
On a Monday or during a
  dark moon

TIME TO ALLOT FOR THE SPELL:
15 minutes

WHERE TO PERFORM THE SPELL:
Altar

INGREDIENTS/TOOLS:
Pinch of cayenne pepper
Black or white votive or
  pillar candle
Lighter or matches
Necklace

1. Cleanse your altar.

2. Sprinkle the cayenne pepper on the top of the candle to anoint it.

3. Light the candle and visualize its mending properties.

4. Move your necklace through the candle's smoke as you say,
   "Necklace of healing,
   fill the void of my broken heart
   as I imbue you with energy and feeling;
   support me in creating my restart."

5. Allow your power to infuse the necklace, charging it for use.

6. Repeat the spell every few months to recharge the talisman. You may use the same candle.

Fidelity Ring Charm

This spell enchants commitment rings to inspire trust between you and your partner. This spell is intended for use on wedding bands, but it can be used on any jewelry.

WHEN TO PERFORM THIS SPELL:
During the spring equinox, summer solstice, or a waxing moon

TIME TO ALLOT FOR THE SPELL:
15 minutes

WHERE TO PERFORM THE SPELL:
Altar

INGREDIENTS/TOOLS:
1 tablespoon carrier oil
2 large plates
Pink pillar candle
1 teaspoon dried basil
1 teaspoon dried licorice root
Lighter or matches
2 pieces of jewelry, one from you and one from your partner

1. Cleanse your altar.

2. Pour the carrier oil onto a plate.

3. Lay the pillar candle in the oil and roll it back and forth.

4. Sprinkle the basil and licorice root over the oiled candle until it's lightly coated on all sides. Focus on setting your intentions into the candle.

5. Stand the anointed candle on the second plate and light it.

6. Take your two pieces of jewelry and pass them through the candle smoke, being careful not to get too close to the flame.

7. Focus on imbuing each piece with thoughts of trust, commitment, faithfulness, and devotion.

8. Let the jewelry cool. Wear the jewelry and repeat the spell every 1 to 3 months to recharge the pieces.

Come to Me Oil

You can wear this oil on your skin to send out energy and vibrations to draw in love or use it to anoint candles, poppets, or charms. If you know that you have sensitive skin, test it on a small area first. This oil will remain potent for around eight months; after that, make a new batch.

WHEN TO PERFORM THIS SPELL:
On a Friday or during a
   full moon

TIME TO ALLOT FOR THE SPELL:
20 minutes

WHERE TO PERFORM THE SPELL:
Altar

INGREDIENTS/TOOLS:
2 tablespoons carrier oil, such
   as almond or jojoba
Small amber roller bottle or
   dropper bottle
2 drops rose essential oil
2 drops cedar essential oil
1 drop lavender essential oil
1 drop vanilla essential oil
Pinch of orange zest

1. Cleanse your altar.

2. Pour the carrier oil into the amber bottle.

3. Add the rose, cedar, lavender, and vanilla essential oils to the bottle one at a time. As you add each ingredient, say, *"Come to me."*

4. Add in the orange zest.

5. Hold the bottle in your hands and envision energy wrapping around it. Charge it with your intentions.

Citrine Sight Potion

This tea potion aids in divining love and seeing visions of your future partner. It can also be used to charge your citrine stone. Citrine assists in stimulating the mind to enhance your visions.

WHEN TO PERFORM THIS SPELL:
On a Friday or during a
   new moon

TIME TO ALLOT FOR THE SPELL:
15 to 20 minutes

WHERE TO PERFORM THE SPELL:
Kitchen

INGREDIENTS/TOOLS:
Small pot
1 cup water
1 teaspoon dried rose petals
1 teaspoon dried chamomile
½ teaspoon dried mugwort
½ teaspoon dried lemongrass
Citrine crystal
Muslin cloth or strainer
Cup for drinking

1. Cleanse your kitchen.

2. In a small pot, boil the water and remove it from the heat.

3. Place the rose petals, chamomile, mugwort, and lemongrass one at a time into the pot.

4. Hold the citrine crystal in your hands and say,
   "With these herbs, I amplify
   and uncover what's unseen;
   with this tea, I clarify
   visions revealed through citrine."

5. Slowly stir the potion as you visualize the energy of enhanced sight wrapping around the citrine stone. Let the potion steep for 10 minutes.

6. Strain the potion into a cup and drink, still holding your charged citrine.

Lovers' Bind Rune

Preserve or attract a loving relationship with the help of this bind rune (for more on runes, see page 30). Bind runes are made by combining two or more runes into a single shape. To perform this spell, find a flat stone that calls to you. You'll use this stone to house your bind rune.

WHEN TO PERFORM THIS SPELL:
On a Friday or during a
 new moon

TIME TO ALLOT FOR THE SPELL:
15 minutes

WHERE TO PERFORM THE SPELL:
Altar

INGREDIENTS/TOOLS:
List of runes and their
 meanings
Sheet of paper
Red permanent marker
Foraged stone or rock, flat
 enough to write on

1. Cleanse your altar.

2. Practice creating a bind rune by drawing two rune shapes on top of one another on a sheet of paper. Choose two runes that represent your intention of love. For relationships and happiness, Gebo and Wunjo are great runes to use. Gebo is the rune of gifts and partnerships, and Wunjo is the rune of joy and pleasure.

3. Purify the stone.

4. Hold the stone in your hand and visualize the energy of your intentions pouring into the stone.

5. Use the permanent marker to write the bind rune on your stone.

6. Carry your bind rune charm with you.

Sweetheart Sachet

Use this charmed sachet to attract a sweetheart. Carry it in a purse or pocket, or keep it under your pillow to dream about a future love interest. You must keep the sachet close to you in order for it to do its work.

WHEN TO PERFORM THIS SPELL:
On a Friday or during a
   new moon

TIME TO ALLOT FOR THE SPELL:
15 minutes

WHERE TO PERFORM THE SPELL:
Altar or kitchen

INGREDIENTS/TOOLS:
Lighter or matches
Red or pink votive candle
8-inch square of red or
   pink cloth
2 teaspoons dried strawberries
2 teaspoons dried chickweed
2 teaspoons dried rose petals
2 teaspoons dried lavender
2 cinnamon sticks
Pink topaz or ruby
Heart-shaped charm or
   Custom Love Sigil (page 47)
Red or pink string

1. Cleanse your altar or kitchen space.

2. Light the votive candle and visualize your intentions.

3. Lay out the cloth. Place the strawberries, chickweed, rose petals, lavender, cinnamon sticks, your crystal of choice, and your charm into it as you say,

   "Strawberry for sweet love,
   chickweed for relationships,
   rose petals for romance,
   lavender for attraction,
   cinnamon for happiness,
   crystal for allure,
   charm for my heart."

4. Pull up the sides of the cloth and tie a string tightly around it to seal the sachet shut, envisioning the energies of the ingredients.

Rose Petal Mist Spell

Charm suitors with this spelled mist. It can be sprayed onto your skin or into the air around you to send out an inviting energy that will attract people to you. You can also spray this mist around your altar to amplify your intentions in love spells.

WHEN TO PERFORM THIS SPELL:
On a Monday, Friday, or during a waxing moon

TIME TO ALLOT FOR THE SPELL:
20 minutes

WHERE TO PERFORM THE SPELL:
Kitchen

INGREDIENTS/TOOLS:
½ cup distilled water or boiled tap water at room temperature
1 (6-ounce) amber glass spray bottle
6 drops rose essential oil

1. Cleanse your altar or kitchen space.

2. Pour the distilled water into the spray bottle and add the rose essential oil. Shake to mix.

3. As you shake, infuse the mixture with your intentions to attract a love interest. If it helps, hold the bottle between your hands and envision your energy wrapping around it and becoming a part of the liquid.

4. Shake before each use to ensure the water and oil are combined. Reapply every few hours.

Desire Incense

Desire incense is perfect for inspiring passion, lust, or strong emotions. Use this in the bedroom or to enhance love spells, such as the Restore Love Knot Spell on page 48. This mixture should be burned on a charcoal disc.

WHEN TO PERFORM THIS SPELL:
On a Friday or during a waxing moon or full moon

TIME TO ALLOT FOR THE SPELL:
20 minutes

WHERE TO PERFORM THE SPELL:
Altar or kitchen

INGREDIENTS/TOOLS:
Mortar and pestle
1 tablespoon dried jasmine
1 tablespoon dried lemon balm
1 tablespoon dried rose petals
1 tablespoon dried damiana
1 tablespoon dried cardamom
Charcoal disc
Heat-proof dish
Lighter or matches
Small glass jar

1. Cleanse your altar or kitchen space.

2. Use a mortar and pestle to lightly grind the jasmine, lemon balm, rose petals, damiana, and cardamom. Let them remain coarse.

3. As you grind the herbs, focus on your intentions and allow your energy to mix with the herbs. Using a mortar and pestle will allow you to infuse a little more energy into the mixture than using a grinder would.

4. Place the ground herbs on a charcoal disc on a heat-proof dish and light them.

5. Save any additional ground herbs in a glass jar for future use.

Lovers' Tonic

This lovers' tonic is a mulled drink that uses kitchen witchery, enchanted herbs, and an intimate setting to bring you closer to your lover. It inspires and manifests passion, trust, and love and banishes shyness.

WHEN TO PERFORM THIS SPELL:
On a Friday, Valentine's Day, or during a full moon

TIME TO ALLOT FOR THE SPELL:
30 minutes

WHERE TO PERFORM THE SPELL:
Kitchen

INGREDIENTS/TOOLS:
Bottle of red wine
1 cup brandy
Medium pot
1 orange, sliced
3 cinnamon sticks
Pinch of nutmeg
Small handful of star anise
6 cloves
2 to 4 tablespoons sugar, honey, or maple syrup
2 cups for drinking

1. Cleanse your kitchen.

2. Pour wine and brandy into a medium pot and heat on low for 10 minutes. If you'd like to cook off the alcohol, boil the mixture for 10 minutes instead.

3. As the mixture heats up, bless it by saying,
   "Bring forth passion, trust, and love with each sip."

4. Add in the orange, cinnamon sticks, nutmeg, star anise, cloves, and your sweetener of choice. Simmer for 15 minutes.

5. Remove from the heat, let cool, and drink with your partner.

Harmony Braid Spell

Do you feel your relationship needs more balance and harmony? Do you feel something is out of alignment in your relationship? This spell uses weaving magic to attract and "braid" together balance, harmony, and love.

WHEN TO PERFORM THIS SPELL:
On a Monday, Friday, or during a new moon or waning moon

TIME TO ALLOT FOR THE SPELL:
30 minutes

WHERE TO PERFORM THE SPELL:
Altar

INGREDIENTS/TOOLS:
3 clear quartz crystals
3 gray or white tea light candles
3 (12-inch) pieces of string or yarn in different colors
Beads in red and pink hues or in your and your partner's favorite colors

1. Cleanse your altar.

2. Place the quartz crystals and tea light candles in a triangular configuration on your altar.

3. Light the candles and focus on setting your intentions.

4. Remove the crystals from the triangular configuration and hold them in your hands. Practice visualizing until you can see the energy that you and the quartz are emitting. Draw on the energy of the quartz to assist you with this spell.

5. Tie the three pieces of string together at one end with an overhand knot.

6. Braid the strings together. As you do this, think about weaving harmony into your relationship.

CONTINUED

7. Every inch or so, add beads onto each of the strings, binding together love, balance, and harmony. Say,

   "String of harmony, intertwine;
   beads of balance, weave together;
   braid of love, bind and connect."

8. Knot the end of the braid.

9. Use the braid as a bracelet or hang it in a shared space.

Seven-Day Love Candle Spell

Do you need a stronger love or attraction spell? In this spell, you'll set aside 15 minutes every day for seven days to focus your intentions on love. The energy amplifies a little more each day, creating a potent love spell.

WHEN TO PERFORM THIS SPELL:
During a waning moon or
  new moon

TIME TO ALLOT FOR THE SPELL:
15 minutes a day for 7 days

WHERE TO PERFORM THE SPELL:
Altar

INGREDIENTS/TOOLS:
Red or white pillar candle
Athame or knife, for carving
  (optional)
Lovers' Bind Rune (page 54)
  (optional)
2 tablespoons carrier oil, such
  as olive or sunflower oil
2 drops geranium essential oil
2 drops clary sage essential oil
2 drops sweet orange
  essential oil
Small amber bottle, for storing
  the oil mixture
Plate
Mortar and pestle or
  grinder (unless using powdered herbs)
1 tablespoon dried lemon balm
  or lemon verbena
Lighter or matches

1. Cleanse your altar.

2. Purify the candle. To enhance the spell, use an athame or knife to carve your Lovers' Bind Rune (page 54) or your partner's initials into the candle.

3. Combine the carrier oil and geranium, clary sage, and sweet orange essential oils in the bottle. As you do this, focus on raising energy for the spell.

CONTINUED

4. Place the candle on the plate and anoint it with the oil mixture. With your hands, rub the oil mixture all over the candle, starting at the top and working your way down to the base. Direct your energy to attract love into your life.

5. If necessary, use a mortar and pestle or grinder to grind the dried lemon balm or lemon verbena. Sprinkle this powder all over your candle. If you'd like, you can keep some powder to sprinkle during the spell.

6. Light the candle, close your eyes, and meditate for 15 minutes, focusing on your intentions. As you meditate, say,
   "Wax of devotion, impart your strength;
   fire of passion, bestow your power;
   herbs of emotion, lend your potency;
   smoke of attraction, grant your energy."

7. Repeat every day for 7 days.

Unwanted Affection Charm

Have you attracted unwanted attention? Do you have admirers you wish couldn't see you? This spell combines a protection charm with an invisibility spell to mask your energy and deflect uninvited interest. Wear this charm whenever you are in the presence of an unwelcome suitor.

WHEN TO PERFORM THIS SPELL:
On a Saturday or during a dark moon

TIME TO ALLOT FOR THE SPELL:
20 minutes

WHERE TO PERFORM THE SPELL:
Altar

INGREDIENTS/TOOLS:
1 cup sea salt or black salt
5 drops lemongrass essential oil
Gray votive or tea light candle
Small mirror
Lighter or matches
1 teaspoon black pepper
Smoky quartz crystal

1. Cleanse your altar.

2. Use the salt to create a small circle symbol of protection on your altar, focusing on protective energies.

3. Put 5 drops of lemongrass essential oil on top of the candle. Do not get oil on the wick.

4. Face the mirror away from you to repel unwanted energy. Keep it facing away from you for the entire spell.

5. Light the candle and sprinkle the black pepper onto the flame of the candle. Say,
   "Burning flame, shield me from affection;
   cracked black pepper, guard me from attention."

CONTINUED

Unwanted Affection Charm CONTINUED

6. Take your smoky quartz crystal into your hands. Say,
   "Shining quartz, shelter me with protection."

7. Close your eyes and pull your energy into the smoky quartz. It should start to feel hot.

8. Clear away your altar items and discard the candle. Your smoky quartz is now charged. Carry it to shield yourself from unwanted attention.

9. Recharge the smoky quartz every few months.

Crystal Grid for Love

Crystal grids use charged crystals placed in a geometric pattern to amplify your power. This particular grid is made up of clear quartz, but you can use any crystal that has love properties, such as rose quartz, pink tourmaline, moonstone, or aventurine.

WHEN TO PERFORM THIS SPELL:
On a Friday or during a
full moon

TIME TO ALLOT FOR THE SPELL:
30 minutes

WHERE TO PERFORM THE SPELL:
Altar or outdoors under the
moonlight

INGREDIENTS/TOOLS:
Pen and paper
4 to 8 clear quartz crystals
Wand or athame

1. Cleanse your altar or outdoor space.

2. With pen and paper, create a grid shape that feels right to you. For love crystal grids, try using two overlapping symbols to represent you and a potential partner. Don't place the crystals in your grid formation just yet—you'll do that in step 4.

3. Hold the crystals in your hands and visualize your energy and intentions mixing with them. Say an affirmation of your choice, such as *"I charge these crystals to attract a loving partner into my life."*

4. Use the crystals to re-create the grid you designed in step 2. Start with one crystal in the center and work outward.

5. Use your wand or athame to activate your grid. Direct your energy to link the crystals together. Say, *"I link this grid to attract a true relationship into my life."*

CONTINUED

6. Sit back, close your eyes, and meditate on your intentions for 10 minutes.

7. Leave your grid in place for as long as you want it to be active. Every few days, link each crystal again and say your intentions out loud.

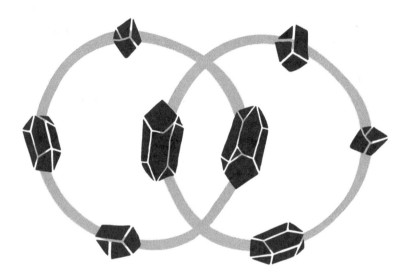

Inviting Romance Spell Bottle

Spell bottles are great long-term spells that help attract or repel all sorts of energies. This particular spell bottle has been created to attract more romance into your life. You can substitute clear quartz for any or all of the crystals in this spell.

WHEN TO PERFORM THIS SPELL:
On a Friday or during a
  new moon

TIME TO ALLOT FOR THE SPELL:
30 minutes, plus 3 to 4 hours
  burn time

WHERE TO PERFORM THE SPELL:
Altar

INGREDIENTS/TOOLS:
Pen and paper
Small or medium glass jar
  with a lid
1 tablespoon dried rose petals
1 tablespoon dried orange peel
1 tablespoon dried basil
1 emerald
1 garnet
1 rose quartz crystal
Photo of your love interest
  (optional)
Lighter or matches
4-inch red or pink chime candle
  or mini taper candle

1. Cleanse your altar.

2. Spend 5 to 10 minutes writing a description of your ideal partner or a love letter to yourself.

3. Place the note into the glass jar and focus on your intentions to invite romance into your life.

4. Add the rose petals, orange peel, and basil. Then add the emerald, garnet, and rose quartz crystals, along with a photo of your love interest, if you wish. Close the lid.

CONTINUED

5. Light the candle and, holding it horizontally, allow it to drip wax onto the lid of the jar. Let wax drip onto the lid until there is enough wax to hold the candle upright. Stick the candle in the wax on the lid, still lit, and hold it steady in place. Allow the wax to dry around the candle so it can stand on its own.

6. While the candle burns, focus on fire scrying (see page 39) with the candle flame and meditate on your intentions. Shapes, messages, or images may come through.

7. Allow the candle to burn out, sealing your intentions into the spell bottle.

Relationship Poppets

Poppets are a fun way to get creative with your spells. This spell directs you to make a set of two poppets, or dolls, to represent you and your ideal partner. Keep these poppets on your altar or tie them together with ribbon and store in a box.

WHEN TO PERFORM THIS SPELL:
On a Friday or during a
  new moon

TIME TO ALLOT FOR THE SPELL:
30 minutes

WHERE TO PERFORM THE SPELL:
Altar

INGREDIENTS/TOOLS:
4 square pieces of red fabric
  (or a color that represents
  you), 2 for each poppet
Sewing needle
Red thread
Polyester fiberfill or cotton
  balls, for stuffing
Pencil
Scissors
1 teaspoon dried
  hibiscus flowers
1 teaspoon dried rose petals
1 teaspoon dried
  jasmine flowers
1 teaspoon dried willow bark

1. Cleanse your altar.

2. Purify the fabric, needle, thread, and stuffing.

3. Sketch the outline of the front and back of the first doll onto two pieces of the fabric. Use the scissors to cut out the shapes.

4. Place the two pieces together with the wrong sides of the fabric facing out. Stitch around the outside of the two pieces to make a poppet. Leave a few inches open and turn your poppet inside out to hide the stitches.

5. Repeat steps 3 and 4 to make a second poppet, representing your partner. If you want to, you can make a larger or smaller doll to represent a masculine or feminine figure.

CONTINUED

6. Stuff both poppets with polyester fiberfill and the hibiscus flowers, rose petals, jasmine flowers, and willow bark. Charge each ingredient as you add it.

7. Sew the openings of both dolls shut. Imbue the completed poppets with intention.

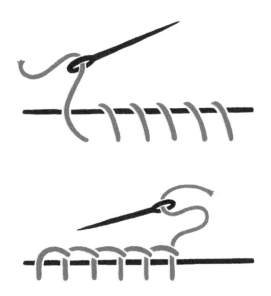

Scrying for Love

Scrying for love will allow you to connect to your unconscious mind and see images of potential partners, relationships, or important messages. A purple candle can enhance your psychic abilities and divination, whereas a red candle assists in manifesting love.

WHEN TO PERFORM THIS SPELL:
During a dark moon or
  new moon

TIME TO ALLOT FOR THE SPELL:
20 minutes

WHERE TO PERFORM THE SPELL:
Altar

INGREDIENTS/TOOLS:
Lighter or matches
Purple candle
Red candle
Dark bowl
1 cup water charged under
  a full moon (see page 38)
Pen and paper
Wand or athame

1. Cleanse your altar.

2. Light the purple and red candles and focus on your intentions to scry for love.

3. Patiently allow yourself to reach a centered, trancelike state.

4. Open your eyes and gaze into the bowl of charged water, allowing any messages or images that come through to fill your mind. Continue to hold your intentions while you gaze.

5. Look for colors and shapes, or listen to messages that come through. Take notes on what you see with a pen and paper.

6. Tap a wand or athame into the water to create ripples, which will help make shapes. These shapes will help stimulate images or visions.

7. Allow yourself time to see images—the more you practice gazing, the better you'll get at seeing them.

Jealousy Mirror Spell

Jealousy can be a destructive emotion. A mirror is the perfect tool to help deflect jealousy, at least in the short term. This spell uses a mirror and a poppet to deflect negative emotions that come your way.

WHEN TO PERFORM THIS SPELL:
During a dark moon

TIME TO ALLOT FOR THE SPELL:
30 minutes

WHERE TO PERFORM THE SPELL:
Altar

INGREDIENTS/TOOLS:
2 square pieces of fabric in a color that represents you
Sewing needle
Thread in a color that represents you
Mirror
Small photograph of yourself
Small box to house your poppet and mirror in
Pencil
Scissors
Polyester fiberfill or cotton balls, for stuffing
1 teaspoon sea salt or black salt
1 teaspoon black pepper
1 bay leaf
1 teaspoon dried ginger

1. Cleanse your altar.

2. Purify the fabric, needle, thread, mirror, photograph, and box.

3. Sketch the outline of the front and back of your doll onto the two pieces of fabric. Use scissors to cut out the shapes.

4. Place the two pieces of fabric together with the wrong sides facing out. Stitch around the outside of the two pieces to make a poppet. Leave a few inches open and turn your poppet inside out to hide the stitches.

5. Stuff the poppets with polyester fiberfill and the salt, black pepper, bay leaf, ginger, and photograph.

6. Sew the opening shut. Imbue your completed poppet with intention.

7. Place your poppet and your mirror in the box and say,
   "With this mirror, I deflect and refract
   unwanted emotions of jealousy.
   With this poppet, I absorb and attract
   unwanted feelings harmful to me."

8. Keep your poppet and mirror hidden in the box, but keep the box close to you.

CHAPTER
4

MONEY
MATTERS

&

PROSPERITY

money and prosperity spells are some of the most popular spells cast today. The spells in this section won't make you rich overnight, but they will help you change your mentality about money, overcome your obstacles related to finance, and invite wealth and prosperity into your life.

Money Powder

This powder is great for improving any kind of financial situation. Sprinkle it around yourself to invite more money to come to you at home, work, or while gambling. You can also burn money powder on a charcoal disc on a heat-proof dish to increase the power of other prosperity and money spells.

WHEN TO PERFORM THIS SPELL:
On a Thursday or during a waxing moon

TIME TO ALLOT FOR THE SPELL:
15 minutes

WHERE TO PERFORM THE SPELL:
Altar or kitchen

INGREDIENTS/TOOLS:
Mortar and pestle or grinder
1 tablespoon dried chamomile
1 tablespoon cinnamon
1 tablespoon dried cloves
1 tablespoon dried parsley
Funnel
Glass vial or jar with a lid

1. Cleanse your altar or kitchen space.

2. With the mortar and pestle, grind the chamomile, cinnamon, cloves, and parsley, setting a specific intention to attract money into your life.

3. As you grind the mixture into a powder, say the following four times:

   "Growing riches, sprouting funds."

4. Use a funnel to pour the powdered herbs into a glass vial.

5. Your powder is charged and ready for use.

Riches Sigil

Creating a custom money sigil can help you attract wealth and riches. To get started with this simple spell, all you need is your imagination, intention, and something to write with. Using a green pen will help elevate your spell.

WHEN TO PERFORM THIS SPELL:
On a Sunday, Thursday, or
   during a waxing or new moon

TIME TO ALLOT FOR THE SPELL:
10 minutes

WHERE TO PERFORM THE SPELL:
Altar

INGREDIENTS/TOOLS:
Pen with green ink
2 sheets of paper

1. Cleanse your altar.

2. Use a green pen to write the phrase *Bring me riches* on the first sheet of paper. Focus on your intentions.

3. Deconstruct the letters of the phrase into basic strokes, like curves, dots, dashes, and lines. Draw these strokes below the phrase on the same paper.

4. On the same sheet of paper, combine the strokes to form the outline of a shape. This could be a square, a heart, a cross, or a triangle. Place any remaining circles, arcs, and dashes along the lines or around the shape. This shape is your money sigil.

5. Redraw your money sigil, now coded with your intentions, on the second sheet of paper. Carry it with you.

Money Grow Dressing Oil

Do you wish that you could multiply your money? You can rub this oil mixture on your skin to help you stay focused so you can improve your finances. Remember to do a patch test first if you have sensitive skin. You can also dress your candles or tools with this oil to enhance the power of other money spells.

WHEN TO PERFORM THIS SPELL:
On a Thursday or during a waxing moon

TIME TO ALLOT FOR THE SPELL:
15 minutes

WHERE TO PERFORM THE SPELL:
Altar

INGREDIENTS/TOOLS:
Small amber roller bottle or dropper bottle
2 tablespoons carrier oil, such as almond or jojoba
2 drops ginger essential oil
2 drops sandalwood essential oil
1 drop bergamot essential oil
1 drop patchouli essential oil
1 bay leaf
1 tablespoon cinnamon chips

1. Cleanse your altar.

2. Pour the carrier oil into an amber roller bottle.

3. Add the ginger, sandalwood, bergamot, and patchouli essential oils, one at a time. As you add each ingredient, chant the phrase *"Money, grow and multiply."*

4. Add the bay leaf and cinnamon chips.

5. Hold the bottle in your hands and envision energy wrapping around it. Charge it with your intentions.

6. Gently shake the bottle before each use to ensure the elements are combined. Use the oil on your skin, charms, or other objects.

Growing Riches Spell

This spell uses Money Grow Dressing Oil (page 78) and a mint plant, which you can buy at any grocery store that sells herbs. Mint is very useful for attracting money and has a variety of uses. A mint plant is a valuable investment for any witch.

WHEN TO PERFORM THIS SPELL:
During a new moon

TIME TO ALLOT FOR THE SPELL:
15 minutes

WHERE TO PERFORM THE SPELL:
Altar or kitchen

INGREDIENTS/TOOLS:
Mint plant
4 items that represent each of the four elements (e.g., a bowl of water, soil, a candle, and a besom)
Coin or money charm
Money Grow Dressing Oil (page 78)

1. Cleanse your altar or kitchen space.

2. Place your new mint plant on your altar and spend time consecrating it. To consecrate the mint plant, pass it through your four elements or ask the elements to assist with consecrating. Both methods utilize your desire to purify, charge, and bless. You can use words or think silently about your goals.

3. When you are finished, anoint the coin or charm with Money Grow Dressing Oil to charge it for use. Place it near the base of the mint plant.

4. Close your eyes and meditate on your intention for the mint plant to grow and attract money.

5. You can pick the anointed mint leaves and carry them as a charm or use them in other money spells.

Money Knot Spell

This knot spell stores and binds your intention to attract money in every knot you tie. You can use any combination of money herbs as incense in this spell, including basil, bay leaf, chamomile, cinnamon, clove, dill, or ginger.

WHEN TO PERFORM THIS SPELL:
On a Thursday or during a full moon or waxing moon

TIME TO ALLOT FOR THE SPELL:
30 minutes

WHERE TO PERFORM THE SPELL:
Altar

INGREDIENTS/TOOLS:
Lighter or matches
Money Powder (page 76) or a powdered blend of any money herbs
Charcoal disc
Heat-proof dish
3 green tea light candles
1 (12-inch) piece of green, gold, or white string

1. Cleanse your altar.

2. Burn the Money Powder on a charcoal disc on a heat-proof dish and arrange the tea light candles in a triangular configuration.

3. Light the candles and focus on your intention of generating more money.

4. Tie five knots in your string. As you tie each knot, say,
   "With knot one, the spell has begun,
   with knot two, the spell will come true,
   with knot three, the spell hears my plea,
   with knot four, the spell grows more,
   with knot five, the spell is alive."

5. Allow the tea light candles to continue burning while you meditate for 15 minutes, visualizing what you want to manifest.

Prosperity Talisman

This spell will consecrate and charge a piece of jewelry with your intentions of prosperity and wealth. This particular version uses a necklace, but you may alter it for any piece of jewelry, crystal, stone, or other pendant of choice. To amplify the spell, use a necklace made with crystal or wood. Wear it under your clothes, hidden from others.

WHEN TO PERFORM THIS SPELL:
On a Sunday or during a
  new moon

TIME TO ALLOT FOR THE SPELL:
15 minutes

WHERE TO PERFORM THE SPELL:
Altar

INGREDIENTS/TOOLS:
Necklace
Pinch of dried mint
White or green votive or
  pillar candle
Lighter or matches

1. Cleanse your altar.

2. Purify the necklace.

3. Sprinkle the dried mint on the top of the candle.

4. Light the candle and focus on visualizing its money properties.

5. Move your necklace through the smoke and say,
   "Necklace I charge with prosperity,
   attract to me riches and wealth,
   and serve me well with sincerity
   while you're worn in secret stealth."

6. Allow some of your power to infuse the object, charging it for use.

7. You may use the same candle to repeat the spell every few months.

Hardship Banishing Spell

With this spell, you can repel a situation that you want to get out of. This spell uses the element of fire to banish hardships that you'll write on a sheet of paper. It can be performed outside over a firepit or indoors in a fire-safe bowl.

WHEN TO PERFORM THIS SPELL:
During a waning moon

TIME TO ALLOT FOR THE SPELL:
20 minutes

WHERE TO PERFORM THE SPELL:
Altar or outdoor firepit

INGREDIENTS/TOOLS:
Pen and paper
Lighter or matches
Fire-safe bowl, if indoors at your altar
Outdoor firepit, if outside

1. Cleanse your altar or outdoor firepit area.

2. Meditate for 10 minutes on your intentions to banish hardships.

3. With a pen and paper, write down what you're banishing. Be as specific as you can.

4. Light the sheet of paper on fire and place it in your fire-safe bowl. If you are performing this spell outside, toss the paper into the firepit.

5. Watch the paper burn and visualize your hardship burning away with it.

6. Scatter the ashes on the ground outside. Say your goodbyes and focus on moving forward.

Income Moon Water Spell

Increase your income with a moon water spell. The full moon is a powerful energy source, which makes this income moon water very strong. Using citrine in this spell can add a boost of energy to manifest stronger results.

WHEN TO PERFORM THIS SPELL:
During a full moon

TIME TO ALLOT FOR THE SPELL:
15 minutes

WHERE TO PERFORM THE SPELL:
Outdoors, preferably under moonlight

INGREDIENTS/TOOLS:
3 coins
½ cup water
Small bowl
4 citrine crystals
Funnel
Small glass jar

1. Cleanse your outdoor altar space.

2. Purify the coins to remove unwanted or old energies.

3. Add the water to the bowl. Arrange the citrine crystals in a diamond shape around the bowl.

4. Place the purified coins into the bowl of water and chant,
   "Glowing moon, charge and infuse;
   glistening coin, be the muse;
   gleaming water, now transfuse."

5. Allow the crystals and water to get a full charge. Then, use a funnel to transfer the water into a glass jar.

6. Your citrine crystals and moon water are now ready. Use the citrine to create a Prosperity Talisman (page 81) or as a charm. Use the full moon–charged water to bless your spells involving plants, offerings, or baths.

Wealth Manifestation Rice

We all sometimes need to manifest some extra wealth in our lives. This spell makes use of rice for its attributes relating to money and prosperity. The roots of this spell stem from folk magic.

WHEN TO PERFORM THIS SPELL:
During a new moon or waxing moon

TIME TO ALLOT FOR THE SPELL:
15 minutes, plus 12 hours to dry

WHERE TO PERFORM THE SPELL:
Kitchen

INGREDIENTS/TOOLS:
1 cup uncooked jasmine rice
2 medium bowls
1 tablespoon Income Moon Water (page 83)
1 teaspoon green food coloring
Paper towels
¼ cup shredded dollar bills
1 tablespoon cinnamon
Large glass jar with a lid

1. Cleanse your kitchen.

2. Purify the rice.

3. In a medium bowl, thoroughly mix the rice, Income Moon Water, and green food coloring, focusing on your intentions.

4. Pour the mixture onto paper towels. Let dry for about 12 hours.

5. In another medium bowl, combine the dried green rice mixture with the shredded dollar bills and cinnamon. Pour the mixture into a large glass jar and close the lid.

6. Sprinkle your Wealth Manifestation Rice around you or carry some as a charm.

luxury Tea materialization Spell

During stressful financial times, brewing a cup of tea can be a useful ritual. With this minty spelled tea, you can transport yourself to luxury. This quick spell can be used anytime you want to materialize luxury in your life. All you need is a bit of mint and some common kitchen items.

WHEN TO PERFORM THIS SPELL:
On a Sunday or during a
  new moon

TIME TO ALLOT FOR THE SPELL:
15 minutes

WHERE TO PERFORM THE SPELL:
Kitchen

INGREDIENTS/TOOLS:
Small pot
1 cup water
1 tablespoon dried mint or
  2 tablespoons fresh mint
Muslin cloth or strainer
Cup for drinking

1. Cleanse your kitchen.

2. In a small pot, boil the water as you set your intentions.

3. Remove the pot from the heat.

4. If using fresh mint, take the leaves in your hands and smack them to awaken their scent. Add the mint to the pot. Let steep for 10 minutes while meditating on your intentions.

5. Strain the tea into a cup. Move your hand in a clockwise direction, and say,

   "I mixed this brew to obtain what I require,
   and filled this cup to secure what I desire."

6. Feel the energy fusing with your tea. Drink and enjoy.

Milk and Honey Money Bath Ritual

Healthy finances start with the right mind-set. This ritual bath can clear away your money worries and fears, allowing a healthy energy to take root. Perform this ritual before any money spell to reset your intentions and energy.

WHEN TO PERFORM THIS SPELL:
On a Sunday, Thursday, or
    during a new moon

TIME TO ALLOT FOR THE SPELL:
45 minutes

WHERE TO PERFORM THE SPELL:
Bathroom

INGREDIENTS/TOOLS:
2 cups whole milk
½ cup honey
Large bowl
Lighter or matches
White pillar candle

1. Cleanse your bathroom.

2. Fill your bathtub with warm or hot water.

3. As the tub fills, stir together the milk and honey in a large bowl, focusing on your intention to revive your finances.

4. Light the candle and set it in a safe location nearby.

5. Pour the milk and honey mixture into the bathtub.

6. Soak in the bath for 30 minutes. Focus on resetting your mind-set about your money. Clear away fears and worries.

7. After 30 minutes, drain the bath and blow out the candle.

8. Perform this ritual as often as needed.

Fortune Apple Pomander Spell

Apples can bring fortune into your life in the form of property, assets, resources, possessions, and prosperity. This pomander spell takes about three weeks to work its magic, and when it's finished, it makes for a strong magical charm.

WHEN TO PERFORM THIS SPELL:
During a new moon

TIME TO ALLOT FOR THE SPELL:
20 minutes on the first day, then 5 minutes every day for 3 weeks

WHERE TO PERFORM THE SPELL:
Altar

INGREDIENTS/TOOLS:
Lighter or matches
Green candle
Wooden or metal skewer
Green apple
20 whole cloves
1 teaspoon cinnamon
1 teaspoon nutmeg
1 teaspoon ginger
1 teaspoon allspice
1 teaspoon orris root (optional)
Small bowl

1. Cleanse your altar.

2. Light the candle while focusing on your intentions.

3. Use the skewer to poke holes into your apple, making sure the holes are large enough to fit whole cloves.

4. Fill the holes with whole cloves. As you do this, say aloud the fortunes you wish to bring into your life.

5. In the bowl, combine the cinnamon, nutmeg, ginger, allspice, and orris root and place it on your altar.

6. Roll the clove-filled apple in the bowl of spices for 5 minutes every day for three weeks. As you roll your apple, meditate on your intentions. This will allow your apple to dry (rather than shrivel) and become infused with your intentions.

7. Keep your spelled apple pomander on your altar.

Cleansing Debt Water

Debt can be a heavy burden. This cleansing water is perfect to help wash away financial burdens so you can move forward instead of backward in life. You can use this water to wash your hands or to draw invisible sigils on your windows.

WHEN TO PERFORM THIS SPELL:
During a dark moon

TIME TO ALLOT FOR THE SPELL:
20 minutes

WHERE TO PERFORM THE SPELL:
Altar or kitchen

INGREDIENTS/TOOLS:
1 cup distilled water or boiled tap water cooled to room temperature
Funnel
Large amber glass bottle
6 drops bergamot essential oil
3 drops cedar essential oil
3 drops patchouli essential oil

1. Cleanse your altar or kitchen space.

2. Pour the water into an amber glass bottle and add the bergamot, cedar, and patchouli essential oils. Shake to combine.

3. As you shake the mixture, infuse it with your intentions to wash away debts. If it helps, hold the bottle between your hands and envision your energy wrapping around it and becoming a part of the liquid.

4. Use this wash before and after paying, opening, and using credit cards, loans, and bills. Shake before each use.

Prosperity Wall Hanging

Invite wealth into your household with a prosperity wall hanging. This hanging uses knot magic to hold and amplify your intentions to attract and magnetize with the elements of earth. Hang it in your bedroom, your office, the center of your household, or your place of work.

WHEN TO PERFORM THIS SPELL:
On a Sunday, Thursday, or during a waxing moon or new moon

TIME TO ALLOT FOR THE SPELL:
30 minutes

WHERE TO PERFORM THE SPELL:
Altar

INGREDIENTS/TOOLS:
Spool of green or gold string or yarn
12-inch stick, foraged from the ground
Beads or metal charms (optional)
Scissors
3 to 4 fresh sprigs of basil
3 to 4 fresh sprigs of thyme

1. Cleanse your altar.

2. Purify the string, stick, and beads.

3. Cut the string into at least 30 pieces measuring about 18 to 22 inches in length. Tie the strings to the foraged piece of wood using simple cow hitch (or lark's head) knots.

4. While creating each knot, say,
   "I unite each string to attract and bring more prosperity into this dwelling."

CONTINUED

5. You may need more strings to fully cover the stick with knots. Leave the very ends of the stick empty.

6. Cut a piece of string one and a half times the length of your stick and tie it to each end of the stick. Use this string to hang your piece on your wall.

7. Focus on your intentions and tie the basil, thyme, and beads and charms (if using) to the strings on the hanging.

8. Repeat this spell every few months to recharge your wall hanging.

Money Envelope Time Spell

This is a long-term money spell that works by offering a coin to the earth and caring for it so you can receive riches in return. This spell takes time and dedication, which paves the way for an even better reward and payoff.

WHEN TO PERFORM THIS SPELL:
On a Thursday on or near a waxing moon or full moon

TIME TO ALLOT FOR THE SPELL:
45 minutes

WHERE TO PERFORM THE SPELL:
Altar and/or outdoor area

INGREDIENTS/TOOLS:
Small coin or dollar bill
Lighter or matches
Green or white tea light or votive candle
Money Powder (page 76) or Money Grow Dressing Oil (page 78)
Seed paper envelope, or any biodegradable container (e.g., egg carton) and seeds

1. Cleanse your altar or outdoor space.

2. Purify the coin or dollar bill.

3. Light the candle, focus on your intentions, and raise energy to place a spell on the coin or bill.

4. Anoint the coin or bill with Money Powder or Money Grow Dressing Oil.

5. Place the coin or bill into a seed paper envelope. If using an egg carton or other biodegradable container instead, pour seeds into it and place the spelled coin or bill inside. If you want to help the magic along, feel free to germinate the seeds before planting.

6. Before going outside, extinguish the candle. Then find a spot outdoors to plant your money envelope.

CONTINUED

Money Envelope Time Spell CONTINUED

7. Cleanse the area. Meditate on your intentions for at least 10 minutes, allowing yourself to connect to the earth.

8. When you are ready, dig a hole and plant your offering as you say, *"I offer this coin and these seeds to the earth in exchange for greater riches."*

9. Care for your offering so it will grow.

Money Spell Bottle

This spell bottle is perfect to invite more money into your life. It's a long-term spell that allows wealth to accumulate over an extended period of time. Place this bottle on or near your altar or place of business for it to do its work.

WHEN TO PERFORM THIS SPELL:
On a Thursday or during a new moon

TIME TO ALLOT FOR THE SPELL:
30 minutes, plus 3 to 4 hours of burn time

WHERE TO PERFORM THE SPELL:
Altar

INGREDIENTS/TOOLS:
Pen and paper
Small or medium glass jar with a lid
1 tablespoon chamomile
1 tablespoon dried basil
1 tablespoon ground ginger
Citrine crystal
Pyrite stone
Clear quartz crystal
Money or money charms (optional)
Lighter or matches
4-inch green, gold, or white chime candle

1. Cleanse your altar.

2. On a sheet of paper, write a letter explaining why you want to attract more money.

3. Place the letter in the glass jar and focus your intentions to draw more money to you.

4. Add in the chamomile, basil, and ginger and the citrine, pyrite, and clear quartz crystals. If you wish, add money or a money charm. Close the jar.

CONTINUED

5. Light the candle and hold it horizontally, allowing some of the wax to drip onto the lid of the jar. Let wax drip onto the lid until there is enough to stand the candle upright. Stick the candle in the wax on the lid, still lit, and hold it steady in place. Allow the wax to dry around the candle so it can stand on its own.

6. While the candle burns, focus on fire scrying (see page 39) with the candle flame and meditate on your intentions. Shapes, messages, or images may come through.

7. Allow your candle to burn out, sealing your intentions into the spell bottle.

money manifestation Crystal Grid

A money crystal grid will amplify your power through charged crystals placed in a geometric pattern. You can substitute clear quartz for any crystal. If you have an abundance of crystals, add in tigereye and pyrite.

WHEN TO PERFORM THIS SPELL:
On a Thursday or during a waxing moon

TIME TO ALLOT FOR THE SPELL:
30 minutes

WHERE TO PERFORM THE SPELL:
Altar

INGREDIENTS/TOOLS:
Pen and paper
8 crystals of the following varieties: citrine, carnelian, aventurine, or clear quartz
Wand or athame

1. Cleanse your altar.

2. With pen and paper, create a grid shape that feels right to you. For money manifestation, many people create a grid of three overlapping circles. Don't place the crystals in your grid formation just yet—you'll do that in step 4.

3. Hold the crystals in your hands and visualize your energy and intentions mixing with them. Say an affirmation of your choice, such as, *"I charge these crystals to manifest money into my life."*

4. Use the crystals to re-create the grid you designed in step 2. Place the crystals where your lines overlap.

5. Use your wand or athame to activate your grid. Direct your energy to link the crystals together. Say, *"I link this grid to attract more money into my life."*

6. Sit back, close your eyes, and meditate on your intentions for 10 minutes.

7. Leave your grid in place for as long as you want it to be active. Every few days, link each crystal again and say your intentions out loud.

Prosperity Oat Soap

A charged prosperity soap is ideal for daily use in the shower or bath to send out intentions of wealth, money, and prosperity. Oats are very beneficial in prosperity spells, and as an added bonus, this soap is moisturizing, chemical-free, and good for your skin. It also makes a lovely spelled gift.

WHEN TO PERFORM THIS SPELL:
During a new moon

TIME TO ALLOT FOR THE SPELL:
30 to 45 minutes, plus
3 to 4 hours to set

WHERE TO PERFORM THE SPELL:
Kitchen

INGREDIENTS/TOOLS:
Mortar and pestle or grinder
¾ cup rolled oats
Sharp knife
1 pound glycerin or milk
soap base
Large heat-resistant
measuring cup
Medium bowl
Wooden spoon
1 tablespoon honey
16 drops lavender essential oil
4 drops bergamot essential oil
1 tablespoon French green clay,
for natural green coloring
(optional)
Silicone soap mold

1. Cleanse your kitchen space.

2. Use a mortar and pestle to grind the rolled oats into a fine powder. Focus on your intentions as you grind the oats.

3. Cut your soap base of choice into large chunks. Place the chunks in a heat-resistant measuring cup.

4. Microwave the soap base in 30-second intervals until it is fully melted. Do not let it reach a boil.

5. In a medium bowl, mix the powdered oats, honey, and lavender and bergamot essential oils. Infuse your energy as you stir and say,

   "Oils, oats, and honey,

   blend together for prosperity."

   Add in the melted soap base. If you wish, mix in green clay for natural coloring. Feel free to customize your soap bar and add in some herbs. (Herbs may turn your soap bar yellow over time.)

6. Pour the mixture into your silicone soap mold and allow it to set, around 3 to 4 hours.

7. Remove the soaps from the mold.

Nine-Day Money Candle Spell

Sometimes money spells require extra time to weave together their magic. This is a simple candle spell that works over a longer period of time. Dedicate 15 minutes every day for nine days to allow this spell's power to grow slowly.

WHEN TO PERFORM THIS SPELL:
During a waning moon or new moon

TIME TO ALLOT FOR THE SPELL:
15 minutes a day for 9 days

WHERE TO PERFORM THE SPELL:
Altar

INGREDIENTS/TOOLS:
Green pillar candle
White pillar candle
2 tablespoons carrier oil, such as olive oil
6 drops bergamot essential oil
1 tablespoon dried basil or mint
Lighter or matches

1. Cleanse your altar.

2. Purify the candles.

3. Mix the carrier oil with the bergamot essential oil, focusing on your intentions to bring yourself wealth and abundance.

4. Place the candles about 9 inches apart on the altar. The white candle represents you; the green candle represents the money you are attracting.

5. Anoint your green money candle by rubbing the oil blend down the candle with your fingers. Start at the top of the candle and work downward to enhance attracting energy. Do not get oil on the wick.

6. Sprinkle the basil or mint on the green money candle to power it.

7. Light the two candles and close your eyes. Meditate for 15 minutes on your intentions and say,

"Candle of capital, come to me;
mint of money, weave and oversee;
today I will it, so mote it be."

8. Day one is now complete.

9. Repeat the spell for 8 more days. Every day, bring the green candle an inch closer to the white candle and sprinkle it with basil or mint. After 9 days, they will unite.

CHAPTER
5

WORK
AND
CAREER

Work and career spells can alleviate stressors and burdens at work or with coworkers. These spells won't land you your dream job overnight, but they will help you build confidence, seek fulfillment, and improve your morale. If you're going out for an interview, starting a business, or working your way up the career ladder, these spells can certainly help you.

Confidence Charm Sachet

This charm sachet will help you attract self-confidence when you're doubting yourself. The crystals and herbs used in this spell all have properties associated with building self-confidence.

WHEN TO PERFORM THIS SPELL:
On a Tuesday, Thursday, or Sunday during a waxing moon or new moon

TIME TO ALLOT FOR THE SPELL:
20 minutes

WHERE TO PERFORM THE SPELL:
Altar

INGREDIENTS/TOOLS:
Mortar and pestle or grinder
1 tablespoon dried thyme
1 tablespoon dried yarrow flowers
8-inch square of orange cloth
Hematite stone
Garnet crystal
Orange string

1. Cleanse your altar.

2. Use a mortar and pestle or grinder to lightly crush the thyme and yarrow flowers to release their aromas.

3. Add the crushed mixture to the orange cloth, focusing on your intention to build self-confidence.

4. Charge the hematite and garnet stones, add them to the cloth, and say,
   "With each stone, I craft and create
   a thriving, self-confident state."

5. Close the cloth and tie it with the string to seal your intentions inside.

6. Your sachet is charged with your intentions. Carry it with you.

Smoothing-Over Powder

Defuse a conflict at work with this smoothing-over powder. It uses calming stones, banishing negativity salt, and herbs with happiness and relaxing qualities. This powder can be carried in a jar, sprinkled around the building where the conflict is taking place, or burned on a charcoal disc on a heat-proof dish at your altar.

WHEN TO PERFORM THIS SPELL:
On a Friday or during a new moon

TIME TO ALLOT FOR THE SPELL:
15 minutes

WHERE TO PERFORM THE SPELL:
Altar or kitchen

INGREDIENTS/TOOLS:
1 tablespoon dried lavender
1 tablespoon dried St. John's wort
1 tablespoon dried meadowsweet
Mortar and pestle or grinder
1 tablespoon sea salt or black salt
Funnel
Glass jar with a lid

1. Cleanse your altar or kitchen space.

2. Place the lavender, St. John's wort, and meadowsweet into the mortar and pestle or grinder, focusing on your intentions.

3. As you grind the herbs into a powder, chant 3 times:
   "Defuse, calm, soothe, and resolve."

4. Sprinkle salt into the herb mixture and combine.

5. Use a funnel to pour the powder into a jar.

6. Your powder is charged and ready for use.

fulfillment Scrying

Are you looking for fulfillment? Fulfillment scrying is a great way to connect with your unconscious mind and see images or receive messages. This spell uses full moon–charged water, a candle for enhancing your psychic abilities, and another candle for fulfillment.

WHEN TO PERFORM THIS SPELL:
During a dark moon or a
  new moon

TIME TO ALLOT FOR THE SPELL:
25 minutes

WHERE TO PERFORM THE SPELL:
Altar

INGREDIENTS/TOOLS:
Dark bowl of water charged
  under a full moon (see
  page 38)
Purple candle
Yellow votive or pillar candle
Lighter or matches
Pen and paper
Wand or athame

1. Cleanse your altar.

2. Place the bowl of water in the center of your altar. Place one candle to the left of the bowl and the other to the right.

3. Light the candles and focus on your intention to scry for fulfillment.

4. Meditate for 10 minutes. Allow yourself to reach a centered, trance-like state.

5. Open your eyes and gaze into the bowl of water, allowing images to fill your mind. Say,

   "Reveal to me the sight unseen,
   and possibilities foreseen."

6. Look for colors, shapes, or messages that come through. Take notes with a pen and paper.

7. Tap a wand or athame into the water to create ripples, which will help make shapes. These shapes will help stimulate images or visions. Allow yourself time to see images. The more you practice gazing, the better you'll get.

Quitting Spell Oil

Is there a project you want to quit or a job you need to leave? This spell will give you the boost you need to make those scary decisions. You'll create a blended oil and herb mixture infused with intention.

WHEN TO PERFORM THIS SPELL:
On a Tuesday, Wednesday, or Thursday

TIME TO ALLOT FOR THE SPELL:
15 minutes

WHERE TO PERFORM THE SPELL:
Altar

INGREDIENTS/TOOLS:
2 tablespoons carrier oil, such as almond or olive oil
Small amber roller bottle or dropper bottle
2 drops rosemary essential oil
2 drops cardamom essential oil
1 drop white fir essential oil
1 drop spruce essential oil
1 teaspoon dried thyme
1 teaspoon dried yarrow flowers

1. Cleanse your altar.

2. Pour the carrier oil into a roller or dropper bottle.

3. Add the rosemary, cardamom, white fir, and spruce essential oils one at a time and say,
   "Bundle of nerves, untwine and scatter,
   let me make these decisions that matter."

4. Add in the thyme and yarrow flowers.

5. Hold the bottle in your hands and envision energy wrapping around it. Charge it with your intentions.

6. Shake before each use. Wear the oil on your pulse points or skin or use it to anoint objects.

Promotion Dream Spell

Don't get stuck in the same job and allow promotions to pass you by. Use this dream spell to create a special pouch for under your pillow and propel your career while you sleep. If you are a beginner sewer, I recommend using stiff felt with an embroidery needle and thread in place of a regular sewing needle and thread.

WHEN TO PERFORM THIS SPELL:
On a Thursday, Sunday, or during a new moon or full moon

TIME TO ALLOT FOR THE SPELL:
15 minutes

WHERE TO PERFORM THE SPELL:
Altar

INGREDIENTS/TOOLS:
Pen and paper
2 (5-inch) square pieces of fabric
Sewing needle
Thread
Polyester fiberfill or cotton balls, for stuffing
1 tablespoon dried lavender
1 tablespoon dried rosemary

1. Cleanse your altar.

2. With a pen and paper, write a note describing what you desire at your job.

3. Place the pieces of fabric together so the wrong sides are facing out.

4. Use the needle and thread to sew around the squares of fabric to create a pouch, leaving a few inches open so you can turn it inside out and hide the stitching.

5. Stuff the pouch with your note, polyester fiberfill or cotton balls, and lavender and rosemary. Focus on your intentions.

6. Sew the last few inches shut, sealing your intentions inside.

7. Place the pouch under your pillow at night. Before bed, ask it, *"What can I do to get a promotion?"* The answer will reveal itself in your dreams.

Workplace Peace Spell

Are workplace politics getting to you? Cast this simple spell to amplify your intention to create peace in the workplace. All you need for this spell is a garnet crystal, gardenia essential oil, and a gray candle. This spell works best when you carry the spelled crystal around your workplace.

WHEN TO PERFORM THIS SPELL:
On a Sunday or during a new moon

TIME TO ALLOT FOR THE SPELL:
15 minutes

WHERE TO PERFORM THE SPELL:
Altar

INGREDIENTS/TOOLS:
3 drops gardenia essential oil
Lighter or matches
Gray votive or tea light candle
Garnet crystal

1. Cleanse your altar.

2. Pour gardenia essential oil on top of the gray candle to anoint it with a peaceful energy. Do not get oil on the wick.

3. Light the candle and pass the garnet through the smoke of the flame to imbue it with the properties of the oil and candle.

4. Place the garnet in front of you and say,
   "Gentle peace, I call on you to find your way.
   Enter my workplace and clear the disarray."

5. Meditate for 10 minutes before extinguishing the candle.

6. Carry the spelled garnet with you to promote peace.

Coworker Communication Spell

Cast this spell to encourage easier communication between you and your coworkers. This spell uses a mirror, an oil blend, and a crystal to strengthen your intentions. Wear the oil on your neck whenever you want to encourage better communication.

WHEN TO PERFORM THIS SPELL:
On a Wednesday or during a
 waning moon

TIME TO ALLOT FOR THE SPELL:
15 minutes

WHERE TO PERFORM THE SPELL:
Altar

INGREDIENTS/TOOLS:
Lighter or matches
Yellow candle
2 tablespoons carrier oil
Small amber dropper bottle
2 drops lavender essential oil
2 drops sage essential oil
2 drops peppermint essential oil
Mirror

1. Cleanse your altar.

2. Light a yellow candle and focus on your intention.

3. Pour the carrier oil into a dropper bottle and add in the lavender, sage, and peppermint essential oils.

4. Hold the bottle in your hands, envisioning your energy wrapping around it and charging it with your power. You've created a communication oil.

5. Place three drops of communication oil on your neck. Look into your mirror and say,

   "As I gaze into the mirror,
   empower my words to be clearer."

6. Repeat as necessary.

Energizing Spell

Are you getting burned out at work? This spell enhances and raises your own energy so that you can stay focused and complete difficult, tedious, or draining tasks at work (or at home).

WHEN TO PERFORM THIS SPELL:
Anytime you need a boost

TIME TO ALLOT FOR THE SPELL:
20 minutes

WHERE TO PERFORM THE SPELL:
Altar

INGREDIENTS/TOOLS:
Pen and paper
Scissors
Fire-safe bowl or cauldron
½ tablespoon dried ginger
½ tablespoon cinnamon
Small glass Jar

1. Cleanse your altar.

2. Write down the tasks you'd like to accomplish on a sheet of paper.

3. Close your eyes and focus on raising your energy.

4. Cut the sheet of paper into tiny pieces and toss them into a fire-safe bowl.

5. Sprinkle dried ginger and cinnamon in the bowl and say,
   "Spices, strengthen and empower my wishes."

6. Light a match, toss it into the bowl, and say,
   "Energy, build until this fire extinguishes."

7. Let the fire burn out and place the ashes in a glass jar. Sprinkle the ashes around yourself when you need an energy boost.

A Spell to Remember

Do you have too many things to remember? Use this simple five-minute spell to help you retain and recollect important details, ideas, or tasks at work.

WHEN TO PERFORM THIS SPELL:
Anytime

TIME TO ALLOT FOR THE SPELL:
5 minutes

WHERE TO PERFORM THE SPELL:
At work

INGREDIENTS/TOOLS:
Crystal
Pen

1. Charge the crystal by leaving it under the light of a full moon. If you do not have time to wait for a full moon, charge the crystal by holding it in your hand.

2. Purify your pen. Close your eyes and envision a white light.

3. Hold the crystal in your left hand and the pen in your right hand.

4. Visualize your energy pulsing and growing until you can move it. Draw on the crystal's energy to assist you.

5. Wrap your energy around the pen, focusing on your intentions to remember.

6. After a few minutes, you should feel a burning sensation coming from the pen. This signifies the energy has been transferred.

7. Your pen is charged and ready for you to use whenever you need to remember tasks or details.

Anti-Procrastination Oil

Do you procrastinate too often? This simple anti-procrastination oil is perfect for you. It can be worn on your pulse points, added to an oil aroma diffuser, or used to anoint tools to enhance your focus and protect against procrastination in the workplace.

WHEN TO PERFORM THIS SPELL:
On a Wednesday or during a
   waxing moon

TIME TO ALLOT FOR THE SPELL:
15 minutes

WHERE TO PERFORM THE SPELL:
Altar

INGREDIENTS/TOOLS:
2 tablespoons carrier oil, such
   as olive or almond oil
Small amber roller bottle or
   dropper bottle
2 drops grapefruit essential oil
2 drops peppermint essential oil
1 drop lemon essential oil
1 drop rosemary essential oil

1. Cleanse your altar.

2. Pour the carrier oil into an amber roller bottle.

3. Add in the grapefruit, peppermint, lemon, and rosemary essential oils one at a time. As you add each oil, say,
   "Drive away delays."

4. Hold the bottle in your hands and envision energy wrapping around it. Charge it with your intentions.

5. When you use the oil, focus on tapping into your intentions.

Creativity Sigil Candle Spell

Do you have a creativity block? This spell is ideal for unlocking your imagination and letting it flourish. It's perfect for helping you work on projects that require a continuous flow of creativity. An orange candle is used because orange is the color of creativity and energy.

WHEN TO PERFORM THIS SPELL:
During a waxing moon

TIME TO ALLOT FOR THE SPELL:
30 minutes

WHERE TO PERFORM THE SPELL:
Altar

INGREDIENTS/TOOLS:
Pen
2 sheets of paper
Knife or permanent marker
Orange pillar candle
1 teaspoon black pepper
1 tablespoon orange zest
Lighter or matches

1. Cleanse your altar.

2. Write the word *creativity* on the first sheet of paper.

3. Deconstruct the letters of the word into basic strokes, like curves, dots, dashes, and lines. Draw these strokes below the word. On the same sheet of paper, combine the strokes to form the outline of a shape. This could be a square, a heart, a cross, or a triangle. Place any remaining circles, arcs, and dashes along the lines or around the shape. This shape is your creativity sigil.

4. Carve or write the creativity sigil on the candle.

5. On the second sheet of paper, write down the projects or tasks you'd like to be more creative on. Place the paper under the orange candle and sprinkle orange zest and crushed black pepper onto the candle.

6. Light the candle and allow the wax to melt onto the paper, infusing it with energy. Spend at least 10 minutes meditating and visualizing yourself opening a door to your creativity. Light the candle whenever you need a creativity boost.

Opportunity Poppet Charm

Use this opportunity spell to attract prospective jobs, offers, or openings to you with the help of a key and a poppet. The key represents the opportunities and the poppet represents you.

WHEN TO PERFORM THIS SPELL:
On a Sunday or during a new moon or full moon

TIME TO ALLOT FOR THE SPELL:
30 minutes

WHERE TO PERFORM THE SPELL:
Altar

INGREDIENTS/TOOLS:
2 square pieces of orange or yellow fabric or felt
Key charm
Orange or yellow thread
Polyester fiberfill or cotton balls, for stuffing
Pencil
Scissors
Sewing needle
1 teaspoon dried chamomile
1 teaspoon dried mint
1 teaspoon dried vervain
Ribbon or string

1. Cleanse your altar.

2. Purify the fabric, charm, thread, and stuffing.

3. Sketch the outline of the front and back of the doll on the fabric. Use the scissors to cut out the shapes.

4. Place the two pieces together with the wrong sides of the fabric facing out. Stitch around the outside of the two pieces to make a poppet. Leave a few inches open and turn your poppet inside out to hide the stitches.

5. Stuff the poppet with the chamomile, mint, vervain, and polyester fiberfill.

CONTINUED

6. Sew the poppet shut, sealing your intentions inside. Imbue the completed poppet with intention.

7. Place the key charm on the poppet and tie them together with ribbon or string. While tying them, say,
   "I link this poppet to this key
   to attract opportunity."

8. Keep the key bound to your poppet. This will send opportunities your way.

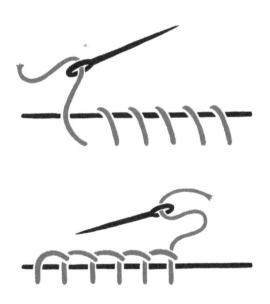

Boosting Productivity Spell

Sometimes a boost is all you need to succeed. This productivity spell can help you balance all aspects of your life so that you can give adequate attention to your work life as well as your home life. When you have too much on your plate, this spell will help you sort through the chaos.

WHEN TO PERFORM THIS SPELL:
On a Wednesday or during a waning moon

TIME TO ALLOT FOR THE SPELL:
15 minutes

WHERE TO PERFORM THE SPELL:
Altar or kitchen

INGREDIENTS/TOOLS:
Small bowl
2 tablespoons water, preferably charged under a full moon (see page 38)
½ teaspoon yellow food coloring
Small glass jar with a lid
2 tablespoons dark corn syrup
2 tablespoons vegetable oil

1. Cleanse your altar or kitchen area.

2. Purify your tools and ingredients.

3. In the small bowl, combine the full moon-charged water with the yellow food coloring. Focus on infusing the water with your intention to enhance productivity.

4. Pour the corn syrup into a glass jar, focusing on laying the foundations for your spell.

5. Carefully pour the yellow-dyed water into the jar to create a second layer.

CONTINUED

6. Pour vegetable oil on top of the water to create a third layer and say,

   "With this brew I infuse
   order with chaos to defuse."

7. Whenever you need a productivity boost, swirl the jar of liquid in your hands and focus on the things you have to get done. Place the jar next to you on the table where you'll be working. As the layers separate, envision the chaos of your own life separating into layers and becoming orderly. Remember to cleanse the jar before each use!

Good Impressions Charm

Do you have an interview coming up? Or do you have a meeting with your boss and want to make a good impression? This spell will assist in creating a positive effect on whoever you wear the charm around.

WHEN TO PERFORM THIS SPELL:
On a Sunday or during a
  new moon

TIME TO ALLOT FOR THE SPELL:
15 minutes

WHERE TO PERFORM THE SPELL:
Altar or outdoor firepit

INGREDIENTS/TOOLS:
Mortar and pestle or grinder
1 tablespoon dried rose petals
1 tablespoon dried lavender
1 tablespoon dried lemon balm
1 tablespoon orange zest
Small glass jar
Funnel
Charcoal disc, if indoors at
  your altar
Heat-safe dish, if indoors at
  your altar
Lighter or matches
Outdoor firepit, if outside
Piece of jewelry, like a ring
  or necklace

1. Cleanse your altar.

2. Use a mortar and pestle to lightly grind the rose petals, lavender, lemon balm, and orange zest. Focus on raising your energy and setting your intentions.

3. Pour the mixture into a glass jar with a funnel.

4. Place the charcoal disc on a heat-safe dish. Light the disc and wait until it glows red. Place a pinch of your newly mixed loose incense on top of your charcoal disc and let it burn. If performing this spell outside, you can throw the herbs into an open flame in a firepit.

CONTINUED

Good Impressions Charm CONTINUED

5. Pass your chosen piece of jewelry through the smoke. Say, *"I bless this necklace to impress."*

6. Imbue the jewelry with the qualities that you feel create good impressions. Be as specific as you can.

7. Wear the spelled jewelry to business meetings and interviews. Repeat this spell on the jewelry every few months.

Clearing a Path Spell

Are you feeling stuck or blocked? Clearing a path is ideal for removing obstacles or stagnant situations that make you feel like you're going nowhere. Use it to kick-start your ideas, career, or projects. This spell uses abre camino and is influenced by Hoodoo.

WHEN TO PERFORM THIS SPELL:
On a Sunday and during a
    waning moon

TIME TO ALLOT FOR THE SPELL:
30 minutes

WHERE TO PERFORM THE SPELL:
Bathroom and kitchen

INGREDIENTS/TOOLS:
Small pot
1 cup water
Handful of abre camino herb
    or road opener oil
Muslin cloth or strainer
Jug or pitcher
1 cup Epsom salt
Lighter or matches
Gray pillar candle
Selenite crystal

1. Cleanse your bathroom and kitchen space.

2. In a small pot, bring the water to a boil.

3. Remove the pot from the heat, place the abre camino in to steep for 10 minutes, and then strain the liquid into a jug or pitcher. Alternatively, you can purchase a road opener oil to bypass this step.

4. Fill your bathtub with warm or hot water and add the Epsom salt.

5. As the tub fills, light the candle and set it in a safe location nearby with your selenite crystal and the abre camino water.

CONTINUED

6. Soak in the bath for 20 minutes. Focus on all the things that you want to unlock and kick-start. When the abre camino water has cooled, poor this mixture over your body to help wash away any blockages and say,
   "With this bath, I wash away
   blockages and disarray."

7. After 20 minutes, drain the bath and blow out the candle.

8. Carry the selenite crystal to heal and balance your energies and ward off future blockages and obstacles.

Responsibility Spell

Do you need help bearing the burden of too many responsibilities? This spell will help ease some of the weight on your shoulders. It uses the Ten of Wands tarot card, which represents responsibilities, burdens, and hard work.

WHEN TO PERFORM THIS SPELL:
An hour before sunset

TIME TO ALLOT FOR THE SPELL:
30 minutes

WHERE TO PERFORM THE SPELL:
Outdoors

INGREDIENTS/TOOLS:
Picnic blanket or something to sit on (optional)
Salt or a wand
Ten of Wands card from the Rider-Waite tarot deck (or a printed image of the card)
Paper and paper

1. Find an area to use as your sacred outdoor space. Cleanse it. If you'd like, set down a blanket.

2. Cast a circle of protection to shield your mind while you meditate. To do this, sprinkle salt or use your wand to create a circle around yourself. Envision white light enforcing this barrier.

3. Sit down and lay the Ten of Wands tarot card in front of you.

4. Stare at the card until you can visualize the scene in your mind.

5. Close your eyes. Allow yourself to fall into a trancelike state, entering the scene of the card.

6. Visualize the character. Are all of the sticks he is carrying necessary? How would you help this character make it to the finish line? Does this character need help? Think of different ways this character could ask for help or offload some of what he's carrying.

7. Return to the present and write down how you can manage or share your own responsibilities. Close your circle, cleanse your sacred area, and reflect on what you've observed.

Motivation Spell Bottle

Do you have the workweek blues? Or perhaps you just need a nudge to get things done. Keep yourself feeling positive with this easy spell bottle. To give this spell an energy boost, use the charged ash from the Energizing Spell on page 109.

WHEN TO PERFORM THIS SPELL:
On a Wednesday or during a
   waxing moon

TIME TO ALLOT FOR THE SPELL:
25 minutes, plus 2 to 3 hours
   burn time

WHERE TO PERFORM THE SPELL:
Altar

INGREDIENTS/TOOLS:
1 tablespoon cinnamon
1 tablespoon sea salt
1 tablespoon crushed chili flakes
1 tablespoon ground sage
1 tablespoon ground ginger
1 tablespoon dried rosemary
1 tablespoon ground nutmeg
1 tablespoon ash from the
   Energizing Spell (page 109;
   optional)
Small or medium glass jar
   with a lid
Aventurine crystal
Lighter or matches
4-inch yellow chime candle or
   mini taper candle

1. Cleanse your altar.

2. Focus your intentions to create motivation and positive energy.

3. Add the cinnamon, sea salt, chili flakes, sage, ginger, rosemary, nutmeg, and ash to the jar.

4. Charge the aventurine crystal, add it to the jar, and close the lid.

5. Light the candle and, holding it horizontally, allow it to drip wax onto the lid of the jar.

6. As the wax drips, chant, *"Motivation blossom, prosper, and thrive."*

7. Let wax drip onto the lid until there is enough to stand the candle upright. Stick the candle in the wax on the lid, still lit, and hold it steady in place. Allow the wax to dry around the candle so it can stand on its own.

8. Allow the candle to burn out, sealing your intentions into the spell bottle.

9. During the candle's burn time, meditate and think about what motivates you and how to hold on to your motivation.

CHAPTER
6

FRIENDS
AND
FAMILY

Your home life and community are important for your social, mental, and emotional health. In this chapter, you'll find spells related to cleansing, purifying, helping, supporting, and building stronger bonds with your loved ones. If you practice ethically, it can be extremely rewarding to use spellwork to help relatives, friends, and partners. Before you perform any spell that involves another person, ask yourself questions about your intentions. Could this spell harm anyone? Does this spell interfere with someone else's free will? You must contemplate these possibilities before you decide whether to perform a spell.

New Home Purification

Moving into a new house is exciting, but you may come into contact with old, stagnant, or negative energy. A blessing for your new home is important for you and anyone you live with. Use this purification spell in your home to hit the reset button.

WHEN TO PERFORM THIS SPELL:
On a Saturday or during a
  dark moon

TIME TO ALLOT FOR THE SPELL:
30 minutes

WHERE TO PERFORM THE SPELL:
In every room of your
  new house

INGREDIENTS/TOOLS:
Lighter or matches
Smudge stick or incense
Fire-safe bowl
Besom or feather

1. Begin in a room at the center of your home.

2. Light a smudge stick and place it in a fire-safe bowl.

3. Cleanse and purify the room by walking clockwise around it, carrying the bowl. Let the smoke fill the room, using a besom or feather to spread it. Say, *"With this smoke, I clear this dwelling and banish all that needs repelling."*

4. Visualize old and negative energies leaving your home.

5. Repeat steps 3 and 4 in each room of your house, starting from the center of each room and working clockwise around the house.

6. Optional: Save any ash leftover in the bowl for protection or banishing spells.

Sweet Dreams Sachet

Create this sachet to promote a restful and peaceful sleep free from nightmares and unwanted dreams for yourself, a friend, or a loved one. This spelled sachet makes for a lovely gift that emits peaceful energy and a pleasant scent.

WHEN TO PERFORM THIS SPELL:
On a Thursday or Saturday

TIME TO ALLOT FOR THE SPELL:
15 minutes

WHERE TO PERFORM THE SPELL:
Altar

INGREDIENTS/TOOLS:
Lighter or matches
Light blue or white votive candle
8-inch square of light blue or white cloth
String
2 teaspoons dried catnip
2 teaspoons dried chamomile
2 teaspoons dried lavender
2 teaspoons dried cedar leaves
Garnet crystal

1. Cleanse your altar.

2. Light the candle and visualize your intentions of peace and tranquility.

3. Lay out the cloth. Place the catnip, chamomile, lavender, cedar leaves, and garnet on it. As you add each item, infuse it with your energy.

4. When you are finished, pull up the sides of the cloth and tie it shut with string to seal it. Say,
   "Dreams be sweet and also kind,
   and leave only peace behind."

5. Sleep with this sachet under your pillow to ward against nightmares. It can also be gifted to a family member or a friend.

Argument Clearing Spell

Do you find yourself often caught in the middle of family bickering? Do you fight with your best friend? Conflicts are often unavoidable, but they should be addressed rather than swept away. Clear the air with the help of a little paper, fire, and intention.

WHEN TO PERFORM THIS SPELL:
On a Wednesday or during a
  dark moon

TIME TO ALLOT FOR THE SPELL:
15 minutes

WHERE TO PERFORM THE SPELL:
Altar

INGREDIENTS/TOOLS:
Matches
Positivity Incense (page 202)
Pen and paper
Fire-safe bowl

1. Cleanse your altar.

2. Light the incense and focus on your intentions.

3. Using a pen and paper, spend at least 5 minutes detailing your argument and your desire to clear the air of your dispute.

4. When you are finished, pass the note back and forth 3 times through the smoke, visualizing your argument being cleansed away while saying,
   "I pass this note through cleansing smoke,
   And banish this argument with each pass;
   I clear the air of any who misspoke."

5. Next, tear your note into tiny pieces and place them in your fire-safe bowl. This discards the argument from your life.

6. Light a match and drop it into your bowl, igniting the note.

Negativity Mirror Spell

Did you catch the negativity bug? Escaping from negativity is nearly impossible. It can come from reading the news, facing daily struggles, or being near others who love spreading negativity and complaining. This spell uses a mirror to protect you from and trap negative energies.

WHEN TO PERFORM THIS SPELL:
On a Saturday or during a waning moon

TIME TO ALLOT FOR THE SPELL:
20 minutes

WHERE TO PERFORM THE SPELL:
Altar

INGREDIENTS/TOOLS:
Compact mirror
Small bowl
4 teaspoons sea salt
1 teaspoon ash
1 teaspoon black pepper
1 teaspoon cayenne pepper
1 teaspoon cinnamon
Permanent marker

1. Cleanse your altar.

2. Purify the compact mirror.

3. In a small bowl, combine the sea salt, ash, black pepper, cayenne pepper, and cinnamon to create a black salt blend with protective properties.

4. Open the mirror above the bowl. Sprinkle a pinch of black salt onto the mirror and say,
   "Little mirror of protection
   guard me with your reflection."

5. On the back of the mirror, use a permanent marker to either draw a pentacle or create a Protection Sigil (page 179). This will trap negative energies and keep them away from you.

Understanding Spell

Walking a mile in someone else's shoes will help you understand their experiences, challenges, and thought processes. This linking spell will temporarily create a connection with another person, helping you get to know and empathize with them.

WHEN TO PERFORM THIS SPELL:
On a Wednesday, Friday, or
 during a waxing moon

TIME TO ALLOT FOR THE SPELL:
20 minutes

WHERE TO PERFORM THE SPELL:
Altar

INGREDIENTS/TOOLS:
Photograph of the person you
 want to empathize with
Lighter or matches
White candle
Turquoise stone

1. Cleanse your altar.

2. Purify the photograph to remove old or unwanted energies.

3. Light the candle and place it next to the photograph.

4. Connect with the energy of the turquoise to power your spell.

5. Envision a white light surrounding the person in the photograph. Create a link with your energy and focus on your intention to understand.

6. Focus on your connection for about 15 minutes, or until you feel your connection is stable and you are able to grasp and understand the other.

7. When you're finished, sever your connection and blow out the candle. The connection has been dissolved.

Halting Ill Intentions Spell

Are you or your loved one feeling victimized? Use this spell to banish negativity coming toward you or a loved one. Banishing is a great way to remove negative or unwanted energy from your life. This spell uses the element of fire to burn away and expel ill intentions.

WHEN TO PERFORM THIS SPELL:
During a waning moon

TIME TO ALLOT FOR THE SPELL:
20 minutes

WHERE TO PERFORM THE SPELL:
Altar or outside

INGREDIENTS/TOOLS:
Fire-safe bowl
Pen and paper
Pinch of dried St. John's wort
Pinch of black salt
Matches

1. Cleanse your altar or outdoor space.

2. Write your intentions on the paper, fold it up, and place it in the bowl.

3. Sprinkle the St. John's wort and black salt onto the paper. Light a match and drop it in the bowl to ignite its contents.

4. Allow the mixture to burn out. Scatter the ashes along the thresholds of your home to protect everyone inside from ill intentions.

Strengthening Friendships Spell

Are you and a friend drifting apart? Revive bonds to make them stronger than ever with this mini apothecary spell bottle necklace. This necklace will help you maintain a calm state of mind and support you in strengthening your friendship.

WHEN TO PERFORM THIS SPELL:
On a Sunday or during a
new moon

TIME TO ALLOT FOR THE SPELL:
20 minutes

WHERE TO PERFORM THE SPELL:
Altar

INGREDIENTS/TOOLS:
Pen
1-inch-square sheet of paper
Miniature spell bottle
6 to 8 dried lavender buds
1 lapis lazuli chip
1 carnelian chip
18-inch jewelry chain or string

1. Cleanse your altar.

2. On the small sheet of paper, draw an intertwining symbol to represent your bond with your friend.

3. Roll the paper up and put it into your spell bottle. Say,
   "With this symbol, I design stronger bonds to pursue."

4. Add the lavender buds to your bottle while saying,
   "Lavender of friendship, realign; create deeper bonds to imbue."

5. Charge the lapis lazuli and carnelian chips and add them to the bottle. Say,
   "Crystals of calm and courage, assign; resilient bonds unveil and debut."

6. Cork the bottle and seal your intentions inside.

7. Put the bottle on a chain or string and wear it as a necklace.

8. Optional: Create a second spell bottle necklace as a gift for your friend.

Respect Palm Stone Spell

Are you feeling disrespected? Turn the tables with your charged crystal to obtain respect through a simple energy manipulation spell. Lapis lazuli is an important stone for gaining respect and is a friendship stone. This spell uses a palm stone or worry stone to create a powerful shift in your emotional state, encouraging self-worth, value, and trust.

WHEN TO PERFORM THIS SPELL:
On a Tuesday, Sunday, or during a waxing moon or full moon

TIME TO ALLOT FOR THE SPELL:
20 to 25 minutes

WHERE TO PERFORM THE SPELL:
Altar

INGREDIENTS/TOOLS:
2 pink roses
2 carnations
2 peonies
3 tea light candles in white, pink, and/or yellow
3 fire-safe plates
Lighter or matches
Lapis lazuli or clear quartz palm stone (palm-size polished oval stone)

1. Cleanse your altar.

2. Purify your ingredients.

3. Remove the petals from the roses, carnations, and peonies. Spread the petals over your altar.

4. Put one tea light candle on each fire-safe plate. Arrange the plates in a triangular formation on your altar and light the candles.

5. Take the palm stone into your hands, close your eyes, feel the weight of the stone, and meditate on your intentions for 15 minutes.

6. As you meditate, feel the energy of the palm stone mix with your own as you relax and center.

New Moon Friendship Spell

New moons are an opportunity to try out new ideas, come up with new goals, and test spells. They're also a good time to attract new friendships. In this spell, you'll write your intentions on paper and use a dressed candle to manifest them.

WHEN TO PERFORM THIS SPELL:
During a new moon

TIME TO ALLOT FOR THE SPELL:
20 minutes

WHERE TO PERFORM THE SPELL:
Altar or outdoors

INGREDIENTS/TOOLS:
Pink or white pillar candle
Plate
1 tablespoon carrier oil, such as olive or sunflower oil
1 teaspoon dried lavender
1 teaspoon sugar
Pen and paper
Fire-safe plate
Lighter or matches

1. Cleanse your altar.

2. Place the candle on a plate. Using your pointer finger, anoint the candle with the carrier oil, starting at the top and working your way down to the base. Do not get oil on the wick.

3. Sprinkle the dried lavender and sugar over the candle. Focus on setting your intentions to attract friendship.

4. On a sheet of paper, write a list of the qualities you want in a friend. Put the paper on a fire-safe plate and place the candle on top of it.

5. Light the candle. Spend 5 to 10 minutes meditating on your intentions and chant:
   "New moon with your glow create
   new friendships to cultivate."

6. Remember to extinguish your candle.

friendship Repair Knot Spell

Do you have a friendship that feels broken? This spell uses knot magic to symbolically build a bridge to an old friend. But remember, this spell cannot force your friend (or anyone) to cross a symbolic bridge.

WHEN TO PERFORM THIS SPELL:
On a Tuesday, Wednesday, or Friday

TIME TO ALLOT FOR THE SPELL:
25 minutes

WHERE TO PERFORM THE SPELL:
Altar

INGREDIENTS/TOOLS:
2 (18-inch) pieces of string in different colors
Scissors
6 small bells with hooks or loops (so they can be strung)
2 pink or white tea light candles
Lighter or matches
2 photographs—one of you, one of your friend
Tape

1. Cleanse your altar.

2. Thread both pieces of string through the first bell. Tie an overhand knot to secure the bell. Focus on your intentions.

3. Repeat step 2 for the remaining bells, tying equally spaced knots down the length of the strings of yarn.

4. Place the tea light candles on either side of you, one to the left and one to the right, and light them.

5. Place the two photographs side by side and tape them together.

6. Jingle your string of bells two times and say,
   "With these bells I banish all hate,
   with each ring I let go and forgive,
   with this photo I bring us together."

7. After this spell, reach out to your friend. Repeat the spell every day. Leave the joined photo on your altar until your bond strengthens.

Blessing Bond Feast

Nothing strengthens bonds better than a ritual feast. Invite your loved ones over to your home to celebrate a sabbat, Esbat or full moon, or holiday. A feast is a great time to give thanks for all that you have in life and honor the relationships you've built.

WHEN TO PERFORM THIS SPELL:
During a full moon, sabbat,
  or holiday

TIME TO ALLOT FOR THE SPELL:
2 to 3 hours

WHERE TO PERFORM THE SPELL:
Kitchen or dining room

INGREDIENTS/TOOLS:
Dishes to share
Drinks to toast
Lighter or matches
White votive or pillar candles,
  one for each guest present
Gifts (optional)

1. Cleanse your kitchen or dining room space.

2. Prepare your and your guests' favorite dishes and drinks.

3. Light a candle for each guest. Place a candle at each place setting.

4. As you await your guests, say,
   "Tonight we will feast, sharing in gratitude.
   Together, we give and share with love and laughter.
   Let all that we do tonight serve the highest good of all involved,
   so mote it be."

5. Welcome your loved ones into your home. Enjoy celebrating with them and allow the candles to burn, imbuing the space with your intentions for a blessed bonding feast.

6. After the feast, extinguish the candles and bury them in your backyard to preserve the results of your blessing.

Popularity Drawing Oil

Is it your first day at school or at a new job? Ease your anxiety and take the pressure off with a popularity drawing oil that will encourage acceptance, recognition, and approval. Wear this oil on your skin or use it to anoint jewelry.

WHEN TO PERFORM THIS SPELL:
On a Monday, Thursday, or during a waxing moon or full moon

TIME TO ALLOT FOR THE SPELL:
20 minutes

WHERE TO PERFORM THE SPELL:
Altar or kitchen

INGREDIENTS/TOOLS:
1 tablespoon carrier oil, such as jojoba or almond oil
Small amber roller bottle or dropper bottle
2 drops jasmine essential oil
2 drops rose essential oil
2 drops sandalwood essential oil
Pinch of dried rose petals

1. Cleanse your altar.

2. Add the carrier oil to an amber roller bottle.

3. Add in the jasmine, rose, and sandalwood essential oils while focusing on your intentions.

4. Add the pinch of dried rose petals.

5. Close the bottle, hold it in your hands, and envision energy wrapping around it. Charge it with your intentions.

6. Allow time to work its magic and make the oil stronger.

7. Wear it on your skin to draw in popularity.

Tower of Trust Spell

Trust between loved ones or friends takes time and effort. It can't be built in a day and won't manifest on its own. With this spell, you'll build a tower that runs in the background to make trust building a little bit easier. It uses an activated crystal to help send your intentions and energy into the world.

WHEN TO PERFORM THIS SPELL:
On a Tuesday or during a
  waxing moon

TIME TO ALLOT FOR THE SPELL:
30 minutes

WHERE TO PERFORM THE SPELL:
Outdoors

INGREDIENTS/TOOLS:
Sodalite stone
8 foraged sticks of
  similar length
Wand or athame

1. Find a flat area to use as an outdoor altar space. Your tower will remain here, so make sure it's somewhere relatively safe, such as a backyard or a balcony.

2. Cleanse your outdoor altar space.

3. Set your intentions. Charge your crystal and place it in front of you.

4. Lay down two sticks on either side of your crystal, one on the left and one on the right, and say,
   "Foundations built to support."

5. Lay down two more sticks across the first two above and below your crystal, making a hashtag or number symbol, and say,
   "Walls built to endure."

6. Lay two more sticks in the same position as the first two sticks and say,
   "Bonds built to thrive."

7. Lay your last two sticks in the same position as the sticks in step 5 and say,

   "Trust built to last."

8. You should now have a tower of sticks around your crystal. Meditate for 10 minutes and imbue your tower with trusting energy.

9. Leave the tower standing as long as you want to build trust.

10. Optional: Repeat the meditation daily to connect with the trust tower.

11. If the tower falls over, repeat the spell.

Acceptance Talisman Spell

Are you stuck in the broom closet? Is there something else you want to share with loved ones, but you're worried about rejection or negative responses? This spell will instill confidence in you, banish anxiety, and improve reception of your situation.

WHEN TO PERFORM THIS SPELL:
On a Monday or during a new moon

TIME TO ALLOT FOR THE SPELL:
15 minutes

WHERE TO PERFORM THE SPELL:
Altar

INGREDIENTS/TOOLS:
Piece of jewelry, such as a necklace or ring
1 tablespoon carrier oil, such as olive oil
Orange pillar or votive candle
1 teaspoon thyme
Lighter or matches

1. Cleanse your altar.

2. Purify the piece of jewelry.

3. Use your pointer finger to anoint your candle with oil, starting at the top and moving down to the base. Do not get oil on the wick. Say,
   "With this motion, I attract courage."

4. Move your finger up the candle and say,
   "With this motion, I banish anxiety."

5. Move your finger back down the candle and say,
   "With this motion, I enhance receptivity."

6. Sprinkle thyme on top of the candle.

7. Light your candle and meditate for 5 minutes about all that you want to achieve and manifest in your life. Imbue the candle with your intentions.

8. Pass the jewelry through the warmth of the flame, imbuing it with the properties of your spell. Say,
"With this motion, I imbue acceptance into this piece."

9. Your piece of jewelry is ready. Wear it to encourage acceptance.

Attracting New Friends Talisman

Are you craving new friendships? Finding new friends can be difficult, and as you age, it can be harder to make new friends. In this spell, you'll work clay with your hands to infuse your talisman with your intentions. This will amplify your energy to attract new friendships.

WHEN TO PERFORM THIS SPELL:
On a Sunday or during a
  new moon

TIME TO ALLOT FOR THE SPELL:
25 minutes, plus baking time
  (dependent on polymer clay
  directions)

WHERE TO PERFORM THE SPELL:
Kitchen

INGREDIENTS/TOOLS:
Carnelian crystal
Oven
Baking tray
Parchment paper
1-inch block of polymer clay
  (pink, white, yellow, or orange)
Scissors
Polymer clay glue (optional)
Skewer
18-inch string or chain

1. Cleanse your kitchen space.

2. Purify the carnelian and set it aside.

3. Preheat the oven according to your polymer clay's directions.

4. Line a baking tray with parchment paper.

5. Roll an inch of polymer clay in your hands until soft. Form it into a ball and place it on the baking sheet.

6. Place a small square of parchment paper on top of the clay ball (to prevent leaving fingerprints). Use your hand to flatten the clay into a pendant.

7. Remove the parchment paper and press the carnelian into the clay. The clay should cover a quarter of the crystal. If you want your pendant to have a polished appearance, paint the clay with polymer clay glue.

8. Use a skewer to create a hole about ¼ inch from the top of the pendant.

9. Bake the pendant according to your polymer clay's directions.

10. While it bakes, meditate on your intentions to attract new friends.

11. Remove the pendant from the oven and, when it has completely cooled, place it on a string or chain. Wear it around your neck or carry it.

Unity Knot Spell

Do you feel misunderstood or misjudged? Are your bonds with your family or friends weak? With this six-strand flat-braided knot spell, you can strengthen your connections with your friends, family, and other loved ones.

WHEN TO PERFORM THIS SPELL:
On a Wednesday, Friday, Sunday, or during a new moon

TIME TO ALLOT FOR THE SPELL:
45 minutes

WHERE TO PERFORM THE SPELL:
Altar

INGREDIENTS/TOOLS:
Lighter or matches
Pink candle
4 (8-inch) pieces of string
Colored beads (optional)

1. Cleanse your altar.

2. Light the candle and focus on your intention to strengthen bonds and relationships.

3. Take the 3 pieces of string, fold them in half, and attach a loop in the middle with the fourth string.

4. Hold three strings in your left hand and three in your right.

5. Weave the outer right strand over its adjacent strand and under the innermost right strand. Put it in your left hand, making it the innermost left strand. You should now have four strands in your left hand and two in your right.

6. Weave the outermost left strand under its adjacent strand, over the third left strand, and under the innermost left strand from step 5. Put it in your right hand. You should once again have three strands in your left hand and three in your right.

7. Repeat steps 5 and 6, weaving in beads if you wish, until you have woven all the string. Your finished piece should be about 6 inches long.

8. Tie another knot at the end, sealing your intentions to strengthen connections and foster unity. Cut any hanging threads.

9. Meditate for 20 minutes and visualize what you want to manifest.

10. Keep your unity braid close to you for as long as you wish to strengthen bonds and bring about unity.

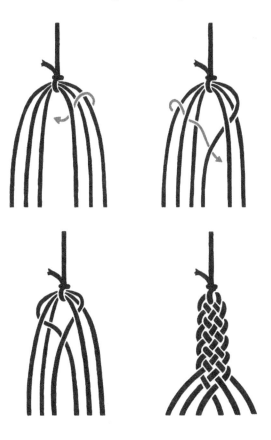

Repairing a Rift Spell

Were you in an argument that escalated? Are you ready to repair a rift between you and someone you care about? This spell will inspire empathy and forgiveness between arguing parties. An important note: This spell cannot change someone's mind—it will only work if both parties are ready to move forward.

WHEN TO PERFORM THIS SPELL:
On a Tuesday, Wednesday, or Friday

TIME TO ALLOT FOR THE SPELL:
30 minutes

WHERE TO PERFORM THE SPELL:
Altar

INGREDIENTS/TOOLS:
2 square pieces fabric for each poppet you plan to make
Sewing needle
Thread
Polyester fiberfill or cotton balls, for stuffing
Photographs of each person involved in the argument, or papers with their names written on them
Pencil
Scissors
1 teaspoon lavender
1 teaspoon cloves
1 teaspoon catnip
Lighter or matches
Blue candle
1 tablespoon honey or a length of string

1. Cleanse your altar.

2. Purify the fabric, needle, thread, and stuffing.

3. Place one photograph of each person from the argument on your altar.

4. Sketch the outline of the front and back of the first doll onto two pieces of fabric. Use the scissors to cut out the shapes.

5. Place the two pieces together with the wrong sides of the fabric facing out. Stitch around the outside of the two pieces to make a poppet. Leave a few inches open and turn your poppet inside out to hide the stitches.

6. Repeat steps 4 and 5 to create a poppet for each person involved in the argument.

7. Stuff each poppet with polyester fiberfill and the lavender, cloves, and catnip.

8. Sew the openings of the dolls shut and place the completed poppets on your altar.

9. Light the candle and meditate on your intentions for 5 minutes.

10. Stack the poppets on top of each other, using honey to stick them together. Honey sweetens feelings and mends conflict between arguing parties. If you don't want to use honey, you can instead tie the poppets together with string.

11. If using honey, store the poppets in an airtight container on your altar to keep insects away.

12. Keep the poppets together until the rift has been resolved.

Spell to Find a Lost Item

Are mischievous spirits playing tricks on you? Did you misplace something? Use this spell to locate any missing objects. To complete this spell, you'll need a pendulum, which is a small weight attached to a length of chain or thread. This method of divination takes practice and concentration. Don't worry if it doesn't work on your first try.

WHEN TO PERFORM THIS SPELL:
On a Thursday or during a dark moon or new moon

TIME TO ALLOT FOR THE SPELL:
15 minutes

WHERE TO PERFORM THE SPELL:
Altar

INGREDIENTS/TOOLS:
Wire
Metal chain or string
Clear quartz crystal
Wirecutters
Pen and paper
Lighter or matches
Brown candle

1. Cleanse your altar.

2. Make a pendulum out of wire, a metal chain, and a clear quartz crystal. First wrap the crystal in wire, coiling the wire tightly so the crystal won't slip out. Then, with the end of the wire, create a twisted loop. Cut off any extra wire and string the chain through the loop. If you already own a pre-made pendulum, feel free to use it.

3. Program your pendulum by asking it questions that you know the answers to. Clear your mind and hold the chain end of the pendulum between your pointer finger and thumb, allowing the pendant to swing. Set parameters: A swing from east to west means yes, north to south means no, and a circle means maybe. As you ask the questions, swing the pendulum in the direction of the answers.

4. Draw a rough layout of your home.

5. Light the candle.

6. Hold the pendulum in your hands and charge it with your intentions. Visualize the lost item.

7. Hold the pendulum over the rough layout of your home and begin asking it questions, like "Is my item located in my kitchen?" Repeat this question for each room of your house. Note the answers the pendulum provides as it swings. Use its answers to look for the item.

CHAPTER
7

HEALTH
&
HEALING

Health and healing spells are intended to help you combat sickness and assist with restoring your mental and physical energy. The spells in this section focus on inspiring change through the manipulation of energy to manifest recovery and recuperation. They cannot prevent you from getting an illness, but they can kick-start your health and defend you from illness. These spells should be used in conjunction with basic health practices such as drinking liquids, eating produce, and getting enough sleep. Healing spells aren't instant—they take time to weave together. Remember to be patient and to never give up on the magic within you.

Seven-Day Health Candle Spell

Feel a bug coming on or a have a stubborn cough that won't go away? A healing candle spell is perfect for you to raise healing energy to combat any illness that is bogging you down. This spell utilizes a blue candle to revitalize and heal.

WHEN TO PERFORM THIS SPELL:
On a Wednesday or during a waxing moon

TIME TO ALLOT FOR THE SPELL:
35 minutes the first day, then 10 minutes daily for six days

WHERE TO PERFORM THE SPELL:
Altar

INGREDIENTS/TOOLS:
Knife for carving
Health sigil (optional)
Blue pillar candle
Plate
Lighter or matches

1. Cleanse your altar.

2. Use a knife to carve the word *health* into the candle. Alternatively, make a health sigil. Follow the instructions for making a Custom Healing Sigil (page 171), replacing the word *healing* with *health*.

3. Place the candle on a plate and light it. Meditate for 10 minutes on your intentions to charge the candle with healing properties. Say,
   "I send this sickness into the flame.
   No more of my health can it claim."

4. Extinguish the candle.

5. Complete the same meditation once daily for a week, burning the candle each time. Repeat as necessary.

Healing Full Moon Water

Water is essential to life. What better way to connect with and honor the life-supporting properties of water than by drinking a magically charged version of it? You can infuse your drinking water through many different methods—this spell uses the energy of the moon.

WHEN TO PERFORM THIS SPELL:
During a full moon

TIME TO ALLOT FOR THE SPELL:
15 minutes, plus overnight
  to charge

WHERE TO PERFORM THE SPELL:
Outdoors or in a window that
  gets moonlight

INGREDIENTS/TOOLS:
3 to 5 quartz crystals
Large jar of water

1. Cleanse the area where your water will be charging.

2. Place the quartz crystals around the jar of water. The crystals will amplify the full moon's energy.

3. Pick up and swirl the jar of water in your hand and say,
   *"Water of life, charge under the full moon's might,
   and imbue and fill with healing light."*

4. Allow the water and crystals to charge overnight.

5. The next day or throughout the month, drink your water.

Cleansing Light Spell

Are you feeling sick, down, or worn-out? Harness the energy of the sun to cleanse yourself of pain, suffering, or illness. This spell combines the energy of the sun with a charm and a candle to kick-start your recovery.

WHEN TO PERFORM THIS SPELL:
At sunrise on a Wednesday

TIME TO ALLOT FOR THE SPELL:
15 minutes

WHERE TO PERFORM THE SPELL:
Outdoors

INGREDIENTS/TOOLS:
Yellow candle
1 tablespoon carrier oil, such as olive oil
1 teaspoon dried rosemary
Lighter or matches
Sun charm or stone and permanent marker

1. Designate an outdoor altar space and cleanse it.

2. Anoint the candle with carrier oil, moving your finger up the candle to banish what you want to get rid of. Don't get oil on the wick.

3. Sprinkle the rosemary over the candle to infuse it with properties of health and healing.

4. Light the candle and pass your sun charm through the smoke of the flame. If you don't have a charm, draw a sun symbol on a stone.

5. Meditate and wait for the sun to rise on your intentions so you can harness its cleansing light.

Healing Bath Ritual

Have a cold that won't budge? Do you feel sick from stress? A healing bath ritual will allow you to hit reset and give your body a chance to heal. This spell uses the healing energy of a blue candle and Epsom salt to relax your body.

WHEN TO PERFORM THIS SPELL:
On a Wednesday or during a
full moon

TIME TO ALLOT FOR THE SPELL:
30 minutes

WHERE TO PERFORM THE SPELL:
Bathroom

INGREDIENTS/TOOLS:
1 cup Epsom salt
3 drops eucalyptus essential oil
3 drops peppermint essential oil
Lighter or matches
Blue pillar candle

1. Cleanse your bathroom.

2. Fill your bathtub with warm or hot water and add in the Epsom salt and eucalyptus and peppermint essential oils.

3. As the tub fills, light the candle and set in a safe location nearby.

4. Soak in the bath for 20 minutes. Focus your energy on the things that you want to heal. Feel the infused bathwater energize your body.

5. After 20 minutes, drain the bath and blow out the candle.

Restoring Flame Spell

Are you feeling exhausted? Do you feel mentally, physically, or emotionally out of alignment? You can use this spell to burn away your (or a loved one's) feelings of weariness, fatigue, or exhaustion by harnessing the element of fire.

WHEN TO PERFORM THIS SPELL:
On a Wednesday

TIME TO ALLOT FOR THE SPELL:
15 minutes per day for the
  duration of the spell

WHERE TO PERFORM THE SPELL:
Altar

INGREDIENTS/TOOLS:
Photograph of the person
  who needs healing
Permanent marker
Fire-safe plate
Blue votive candle
1 teaspoon ground sage
Lighter or matches

1. Cleanse your altar.

2. Use a permanent marker to circle areas of the person in the photograph that need healing energy. For mental exhaustion, circle the head; for emotional exhaustion, circle the heart; and so on.

3. Lay the photograph on a fire-safe plate. Place the candle on top of it.

4. Sprinkle the sage onto the candle as you raise your energy.

5. Light the candle and allow it to burn for 15 minutes. Close your eyes and focus on restoration and healing.

6. Repeat this spell daily until the candle burns out.

Heal Your Sickness While You Sleep Sachet

Too sick to raise enough energy to heal yourself? Heal while you sleep. This herbal sachet is quick and simple to make, and you can stay sound asleep while it works its magic to absorb your ailments.

WHEN TO PERFORM THIS SPELL:
On a Wednesday or during a waning moon

TIME TO ALLOT FOR THE SPELL:
10 minutes plus overnight

WHERE TO PERFORM THE SPELL:
Altar

INGREDIENTS/TOOLS:
8-inch square of blue cloth
2 teaspoons dried chamomile
2 teaspoons sandalwood chips
2 teaspoons cayenne pepper
2 teaspoons dried rosemary
Blue string

1. Cleanse your altar.

2. Lay out the cloth. Place the chamomile, sandalwood chips, cayenne pepper, and rosemary on the cloth one by one and say,
   "I am stronger than I think,
   and with this charm I create a link
   to be restored from a sleep-
   ing wink."

3. Pull up the sides of the cloth and tie the string around it tightly to seal it shut, envisioning the energies of the ingredients.

4. Before you go to bed, breathe in the sachet's scent and visualize yourself healing. Lay the sachet next to you or under your pillow while you sleep.

5. Repeat step 4 at night whenever you are sick.

Healing Moon Talisman

Allow the energy of a full moon to heal you. In this spell, you'll create a charged necklace to amplify your healing intentions. Using a necklace made with crystal or wood can amplify the strength of this spell. If you don't have a necklace, you can use wire attached to a piece of wood or crystal to make a pendant.

WHEN TO PERFORM THIS SPELL:
During a full moon

TIME TO ALLOT FOR THE SPELL:
15 minutes, plus overnight

WHERE TO PERFORM THE SPELL:
Altar

INGREDIENTS/TOOLS:
White or blue votive or
   pillar candle
2 drops eucalyptus essential oil
Lighter or matches
Necklace made with wood or
   crystal (or a wood or crystal
   pendant)

1. Cleanse your altar.

2. Anoint the candle with eucalyptus essential oil. Don't get any oil on the wick.

3. Light the candle and focus on visualizing healing energy.

4. Move the necklace through the warmth of the smoke and say,

   "Necklace I imbue with healing light,
   charge under the full moon's might,
   protect me from sickness after tonight."

5. Hold the necklace in your hands and feel your energy mix with the necklace. Wear it when you need healing energy.

6. Extinguish the candle and place the talisman in a windowsill that gets moonlight.

7. Recharge your talisman during each full moon.

Body Vitality Butter

Return your body to vitality after illness or suffering. This all-purpose healing body butter can be used on aches, bruises, scrapes, dry skin, or rashes. It also makes a great gift for friends and loved ones.

WHEN TO PERFORM THIS SPELL:
On a Wednesday or during a new moon

TIME TO ALLOT FOR THE SPELL:
1 hour and 40 minutes

WHERE TO PERFORM THE SPELL:
Kitchen

INGREDIENTS/TOOLS:
Double boiler or small and medium pots and a ceramic bowl
1 cup shea or cocoa butter
½ cup coconut oil
½ cup carrier oil, such as almond oil
20 drops lavender essential oil
Hand mixer or whisk
Medium glass jar with a lid

1. Cleanse your kitchen space.

2. Heat a double boiler on the stove over medium heat. If you don't have a double boiler, fill a medium pot with water and submerge a ramekin or ceramic dish upside down in the pot, ensuring ¼ inch of the dish sticks out above the water. Place a smaller pot on top of the submerged dish. Do not allow it to touch the water.

3. Combine the shea butter, coconut oil, and carrier oil in the double boiler or add them to the smaller pot, stirring constantly until melted. Remove the mixture from the heat and cool for 1 minute.

4. Add the lavender essential oil and focus on your intentions as you stir it in. Refrigerate the mixture for 1 hour.

5. Remove the mixture from the fridge and use a hand mixer or whisk to beat until fluffy. Return the mixture to the refrigerator for 15 minutes to set.

6. Seal it in a glass jar. Store at around 75 degrees Fahrenheit.

Eucalyptus Clear Out Oil

Clear out coughs, colds, and phlegm with this herbal oil balm. This simple, quick spell uses eucalyptus, a popular remedy for colds and respiratory ailments. If you have sensitive skin, remember to do a patch test.

WHEN TO PERFORM THIS SPELL:
On a Wednesday or during a
new moon or waxing moon

TIME TO ALLOT FOR THE SPELL:
20 minutes

WHERE TO PERFORM THE SPELL:
Kitchen

INGREDIENTS/TOOLS:
2 tablespoons coconut oil
1.5-ounce glass jar with a lid
6 drops eucalyptus essential oil

1. Cleanse your kitchen space.

2. Place the coconut oil in a glass jar. If the coconut oil is solid, microwave on low at 10-second intervals until melted. Be careful not to boil it.

3. Add eucalyptus essential oil to the jar, focusing on your intentions.

4. Stir the mixture and say,
   "With these oils, I infuse
   healing energy for the chest.
   Clear out these sickly blues;
   hear me and grant this request."

5. Refrigerate the mixture until it solidifies.

6. To use, apply a few drops on your pressure points.

Grounding Anxiety Spell

Anxiety can sneak into anyone's life, so it's important to learn ways to grapple with it before it spirals out of control. You already have the power to control your anxiety. Tap into that power with this grounding spell, which requires only a citrine crystal.

WHEN TO PERFORM THIS SPELL:
Anytime

INGREDIENTS/TOOLS:
Citrine crystal

TIME TO ALLOT FOR THE SPELL:
15 minutes

WHERE TO PERFORM THE SPELL:
Altar

1. Cleanse your altar.

2. Get into a comfortable position and hold the citrine crystal in your dominant hand. Close your eyes.

3. Breathe deeply. Visualize an orb of healing light at the top of your head. Feel it move through you, pulling the anxiety out of your body as it makes its way to the base of your spine.

4. When you feel that the orb has collected all your anxiety, visualize sending it out of your body and into the ground.

Reboot Potion

Do you ever get sick and wish your body had a restart button? This spell uses the new moon and a bloodstone to give you just that. Use this spell to shut yourself down and start yourself up again so you're ready to take on the month ahead.

WHEN TO PERFORM THIS SPELL:
During a new moon

TIME TO ALLOT FOR THE SPELL:
30 minutes

WHERE TO PERFORM THE SPELL:
Altar or kitchen

INGREDIENTS/TOOLS:
1 quart (4 cups) distilled water or boiled water cooled to room temperature
Large glass jar with a lid
1 tablespoon dried nettle
1 tablespoon dried vervain
Bloodstone
Muslin cloth or strainer
Cup for drinking (optional)

1. Cleanse your altar or kitchen space.

2. Pour the water into a large glass jar.

3. Add the nettle and vervain and seal the jar.

4. Place the bloodstone on the jar's lid to infuse its energy to aid in rebooting.

5. Close your eyes and focus on your intentions under the new moon.

6. Let your potion brew overnight.

7. Strain and drink the potion or pour it outside your home to surround yourself with the energy of the new moon.

Crystal Grid for Healing Pain

Pain comes in many forms—physical, mental, and emotional. Crystals can help you manage pain by giving you healing and restorative energy. This healing grid makes use of a variety of crystals with healing properties.

WHEN TO PERFORM THIS SPELL:
During a new moon or
full moon

TIME TO ALLOT FOR THE SPELL:
30 minutes

WHERE TO PERFORM THE SPELL:
Altar or outdoors under the
moonlight

INGREDIENTS/TOOLS:
Pen and paper
4 clear quartz crystals
3 citrine crystals
3 turquoise stones
3 peridot crystals
Wand or athame

1. Cleanse your altar or outdoor space.

2. With pen and paper, create a grid shape that feels right to you. Don't place the crystals in your grid formation just yet—you'll do that in step 4.

3. Hold the crystals in your hands and visualize your energy and intentions mixing with them. Say an affirmation such as *"I charge these crystals to heal and absorb my pain."*

4. Use the crystals to re-create the grid you designed in step 2. Start with one large crystal in the center and work outward.

5. Use your wand or athame to activate your grid. Direct your energy to link the crystals together. Say, *"I link this grid to banish pain and protect against hurt."*

6. Sit back, close your eyes, and meditate on your intentions for 15 minutes.

CONTINUED

7. Leave your grid in place for as long as you want it to be active. Every few days, link each crystal again and say your intentions out loud.

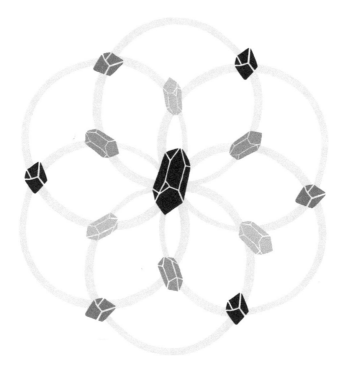

Healing Poppet Charm

Poppets are a tool of sympathetic magic, which makes them ideal to use in combination with prescribed or preventative health care. A poppet can create a connection to you to assist you in your intentions. This poppet is also perfect for using on loved ones to inspire healing.

WHEN TO PERFORM THIS SPELL:
On a Sunday or during a new moon or full moon

TIME TO ALLOT FOR THE SPELL:
30 minutes

WHERE TO PERFORM THE SPELL:
Altar

INGREDIENTS/TOOLS:
2 square pieces of blue fabric
Sewing needle
Thread
Polyester fiberfill or cotton balls, for stuffing
Pencil
Scissors
1 teaspoon dried lemon balm
1 teaspoon dried calendula
1 teaspoon black pepper
Small item that belongs to you

1. Cleanse your altar.

2. Purify the fabric, needle, thread, and stuffing.

3. Sketch the outline of the front and back of the doll on the fabric. Use scissors to cut out the shapes.

4. Place the two pieces together with the wrong sides of the fabric facing out. Stitch around the outside of the two pieces to make a poppet. Leave a few inches open and turn your poppet inside out to hide the stitches.

5. Stuff the poppet with polyester fiberfill, lemon balm, calendula, and black pepper. Charge each item as you add it.

6. Add in a belonging that ties the poppet to you. This can be a strand of your hair, an old clip or bow, or something you've used. Sew the poppet shut.

CONTINUED

7. Place the poppet on your altar. Focus your energy on the part of your body you'd like to heal. Feel your energy wrapping around that part of the doll. Allow yourself to enter a trancelike state for 10 minutes and say,

   "Healing light wrap around,
   restoring energy to surround."

8. Repeat step 7 on your poppet whenever you need healing energy.

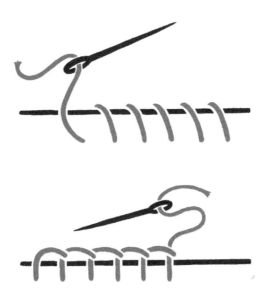

Healing Mirror Spell

A mirror can add a little boost to strengthen your healing spells. This robust spell makes use of a mirror, crystals, a blue candle, and rosemary essential oil to create healing energy for you or a loved one.

WHEN TO PERFORM THIS SPELL:
During a full moon

TIME TO ALLOT FOR THE SPELL:
35 minutes

WHERE TO PERFORM THE SPELL:
Altar

INGREDIENTS/TOOLS:
Handheld mirror
Large fire-safe plate
Pen and paper
Blue pillar candle
3 drops rosemary essential oil
4 quartz crystals or other healing stones
Lighter or matches
Athame or wand

1. Cleanse your altar.

2. Lay your mirror face up on a large fire-safe plate on your altar.

3. Write down the name of the person who needs healing.

4. Place the paper on top of the mirror. If necessary, fold the paper so it fits.

5. Place the candle on the paper and mirror. Anoint the candle with rosemary essential oil and focus on your intentions. Don't get any oil on the wick.

6. Place the quartz crystals around the mirror, paper, and candle in a diamond shape that represents north, south, east, and west, honoring the four elements.

7. Light the candle and meditate for 10 minutes on your desires and intentions.

CONTINUED

8. Open your eyes. Use a wand or athame to point at each crystal, moving in a clockwise direction. Say,

   "With this candle I cast away
   all illness and dismay.
   With these crystals I unite
   and banish all sickness tonight.
   With this mirror I expand,
   amplifying healing energy I command."

9. Allow the candle to burn while you meditate for 20 minutes on your intentions, raising energy for your spell. Let the wax drip onto the paper and mirror.

10. Bury your candle and the sheet of paper.

Distance Healing Spell

If you are far away from loved ones who need healing (or far away from home), you can try distant or remote healing. The method in this spell is sometimes called healing medicine or Reiki and can be done with crystal wands or palm stones.

WHEN TO PERFORM THIS SPELL:
On a Wednesday or during a waxing moon

TIME TO ALLOT FOR THE SPELL:
45 minutes

WHERE TO PERFORM THE SPELL:
Anywhere you can get comfortable

INGREDIENTS/TOOLS:
Pillow or meditation cushion (optional)
Lighter or matches
Purple candle
Crystal wand (use clear quartz, rose quartz, or selenite)

1. Cleanse the space you'll be performing the distance healing in.

2. If you have a pillow or meditation cushion, sit on it to get comfortable.

3. Light the candle to enhance your psychic abilities and help you focus on your intention to heal.

4. Loosely hold your crystal wand in your dominant hand and connect with its energy. Open your other hand with your palm facing up.

5. Close your eyes and practice deep breathing until you reach a meditative state.

6. Channel your energy and push and pull it until you are able to move it in the direction of the crystal. Allow it to connect and merge with the crystal's energy.

CONTINUED

Distance Healing Spell CONTINUED

7. Picture the person you want to bestow healing energy on.

8. Move the wand back and forth, envisioning the healing energy washing over the person you are healing. Focus on your intentions.

9. When you are finished, ground any excess energy and practice deep breathing until you feel your energy center itself again.

Custom Healing Sigil

Make a custom healing sigil to use in a variety of healing spells. You can carve it into healing candles, draw it on stones, or sew it onto poppets or charm bags. Don't worry about making your sigil perfect—the important thing is that it's unique to you.

WHEN TO PERFORM THIS SPELL:
On a Wednesday or during a new moon

TIME TO ALLOT FOR THE SPELL:
10 minutes

WHERE TO PERFORM THE SPELL:
Altar

INGREDIENTS/TOOLS:
Permanent marker with blue ink
Sheet of paper
Flat stone or piece of wood (optional)
Lavender incense or a besom (optional)

1. Cleanse your altar.

2. Focus on your intentions. Write the word *healing* or a similar word on a sheet of paper.

3. Deconstruct the letters of the word into their basic strokes, like curves, dots, dashes, and lines. Draw these strokes below the word on the same paper.

4. Still on the same sheet of paper, combine the strokes to form the outline of a shape. This shape is your healing sigil.

5. Redraw your healing sigil, now coded with your intentions, on the same sheet of paper.

6. To make a healing sigil talisman, draw the sigil on a stone or piece of wood. Light incense and cleanse your talisman by passing it through the smoke. Alternatively, use a besom. Hold the talisman in your hands and focus on your intentions to consecrate it, activating it for use.

Healing Energy Pouch

This healing pouch can be used for physical, emotional, or spiritual healing whenever you feel that you need a boost. The color blue, which is associated with healing, is used throughout this spell: in the pouch fabric, the candle, and the crystal.

WHEN TO PERFORM THE SPELL:
On a Monday or Sunday

TIME TO ALLOT FOR THE SPELL:
3 to 5 hours, depending on your candle's burn time

WHERE TO PERFORM THE SPELL:
Altar

INGREDIENTS/TOOLS:
2 (5-inch) square pieces of blue fabric
Sewing needle
Blue thread
Lighter or matches
Blue tea light candle
4 cloves
4 fresh rose petals
1 blue crystal or stone of your choosing (if you do not have this, substitute clear quartz crystal)

1. Cleanse your altar.

2. Place the pieces of fabric together so the wrong sides are facing out.

3. Use the needle and thread to sew around the squares of fabric to create a pouch, leaving a few inches open so you can turn it inside out and hide the stitching.

4. Light the candle, sit quietly, and imagine that you are well.

5. Place the cloves, rose petals, and crystal in your pouch one at a time and say,
   "With these cloves, I heal.
   With these rose petals, I heal.
   With this stone, I heal."

6. Sew the last few inches shut, sealing your intentions inside.

7. Close your eyes and envision a blue healing energy coming from the pouch and enveloping your body.

8. Either allow your candle to burn out or snuff it out, feeling it take your illness with it. Do not use the candle for anything else.

CHAPTER
8

PROTECTION
AND
FORGIVENESS

Whether you're a new witch or an experienced one, protection and forgiveness spells are crucial to learn. Protection magic, one of the oldest forms of spellcasting, helps us defend ourselves. Forgiveness magic allows us to live in the present and find inner peace. These two types of magic go hand in hand because both are crucial to attaining a sense of safety. The spells in this section will teach you to protect and find peace with yourself, your home, and the people around you.

Home Protection Wash

Protection begins at home. Use this protection wash to shield and fortify your home from malevolent spirits, unwanted attention, and other harm. You should make a fresh protection wash at the beginning of a new season to ensure its potency.

WHEN TO PERFORM THIS SPELL:
On a Saturday or during a dark moon

TIME TO ALLOT FOR THE SPELL:
10 minutes plus cleaning time

WHERE TO PERFORM THE SPELL:
Kitchen

INGREDIENTS/TOOLS:
1 quart (4 cups) water
Large pot
Bucket
1 cup white vinegar
12 drops bergamot essential oil
12 drops geranium essential oil
Washcloth

1. Cleanse your kitchen space.

2. Boil a large pot of water to remove any impurities. Pour the purified water into a clean bucket.

3. Add the white vinegar to the bucket.

4. Focus on your intentions and pour in the bergamot and geranium essential oils.

5. Stir the bucket three times and say,
   "Thrice around the bucket round,
   protect the walls and the ground."

6. Use this spelled wash to clean the windows and doors in your home.

Boundary Protection Salt

Do you feel your boundaries being crossed by unwanted energy or spirits? Take charge and overcome your fear with a batch of boundary protection salt. Use this spell to create a barrier around your home, protecting yourself from undesirable forces.

WHEN TO PERFORM THIS SPELL:
On a Saturday or during a
    new moon

TIME TO ALLOT FOR THE SPELL:
15 minutes plus sprinkling time

WHERE TO PERFORM THE SPELL:
Altar or kitchen

INGREDIENTS/TOOLS:
1 cup table salt
12-ounce glass jar with a lid
1 teaspoon dried basil
1 teaspoon ground cloves
1 teaspoon ground cumin
1 teaspoon black pepper
1 teaspoon ash from a
    previous spell

1. Cleanse your altar or kitchen space.

2. Add the salt to a jar.

3. Then add the basil, cloves, cumin, black pepper, and ash. As you add them, say,
   "Basil to defend,
   cloves to guard,
   cumin to shelter,
   pepper to shield,
   ash to protect."

4. Close the jar and shake to mix.

5. Pour the salt mixture in an unbroken line around your house. Check often to see that the line of salt isn't broken. If the line breaks, repeat the spell.

Protection Amulet

A protective amulet can increase your body's own protective defensive energy. This spell uses the protective associations of the color black (or brown) as well as the protective herb cumin. Wear this amulet or gift it to someone you'd like to protect.

WHEN TO PERFORM THIS SPELL:
On a Saturday or during a
full moon

TIME TO ALLOT FOR THE SPELL:
15 minutes

WHERE TO PERFORM THE SPELL:
Altar

INGREDIENTS/TOOLS:
1 pinch cumin
Black or brown votive candle
Lighter or matches
Necklace or amulet

1. Cleanse your altar.

2. Sprinkle the cumin on the top of the candle to anoint it.

3. Light the anointed candle and visualize its protective properties.

4. Move the necklace or amulet through the candle's smoke and say,
   "Necklace of protection,
   charge with my intention
   and shield in my direction."

5. Allow your power to infuse the amulet, charging it for use.

6. Use the same candle to repeat the spell every few months to recharge the protective amulet.

Protection Sigil

In this spell, you'll create a sigil that you can use on a protection stone. This sigil is also perfect to use along with your Home Protection Wash (page 176)—just dip your fingers in the wash and draw invisible protection sigils on your mirrors and windows.

WHEN TO PERFORM THIS SPELL:
On a Saturday or during a
   new moon

TIME TO ALLOT FOR THE SPELL:
10 minutes

WHERE TO PERFORM THE SPELL:
Altar

INGREDIENTS/TOOLS:
Pen and paper
Black permanent marker
Flat stone (optional)

1. Cleanse your altar.

2. Focus on your intentions. Write the word *protect* on a sheet of paper.

3. Deconstruct the letters of the word into their basic strokes, like curves, dots, dashes, and lines. Draw these strokes below the word on the same paper.

4. Still on the same sheet of paper, combine the strokes to form the outline of a shape. This could be a square, a heart, a cross, or a triangle. Place any remaining circles, arcs, and dashes along the lines or around the shape. This shape is your protection sigil.

5. If you would like, draw your sigil, now coded with your intentions, on a stone to carry with you.

Iron Protection Spell

Iron is an important protective metal, and it's also extremely abundant. It is found throughout the earth and in the stars. Iron is used in magic in the form of nails, horseshoes, and hematite. In this spell, you'll place iron back into the earth as an offering in exchange for protection.

WHEN TO PERFORM THIS SPELL:
On a Saturday or during a new moon or waxing moon

TIME TO ALLOT FOR THE SPELL:
20 minutes

WHERE TO PERFORM THE SPELL:
Altar and outdoors

INGREDIENTS/TOOLS:
Mortar and pestle or grinder
1 dried bay leaf
1 teaspoon cinnamon
1 teaspoon salt
Lighter or matches
Charcoal disc
Heat-proof dish
5 pieces of iron (e.g., iron nails or hematite stones)

1. Cleanse your altar.

2. Use a mortar and pestle or grinder to combine the bay leaf, cinnamon, and salt to create an incense mixture. Set aside.

3. Light the charcoal disc on a heat-proof dish and burn until it glows red.

4. Sprinkle a pinch of the incense mixture onto the charcoal disc.

5. Pass the pieces of iron through the smoke, focusing on your intentions.

6. Meditate for 10 minutes and extinguish the incense.

7. Bury the charged iron pieces around your property to offer the iron back to the earth.

Forgiveness Bath Ritual

Forgiveness isn't instant—it is a process that takes time. This ritual bath will help you start to let go of past trauma, grief, and pain, and it will support you as you forgive those who have hurt you.

WHEN TO PERFORM THIS SPELL:
On a Sunday, Monday, or during a new moon

TIME TO ALLOT FOR THE SPELL:
45 minutes

WHERE TO PERFORM THE SPELL:
Bathroom

INGREDIENTS/TOOLS:
1 cup Epsom salt
Lighter or matches
Black or white pillar candle
3 drops jasmine essential oil
3 drops chamomile essential oil

1. Cleanse your bathroom.

2. Fill your bathtub with hot water and add the Epsom salts.

3. Light the candle and set in a safe location nearby while focusing on your intentions.

4. Once the bath is filled, add the jasmine and chamomile essential oils and get in.

5. Soak in the bath for 30 minutes and envision all your pain and grief being pulled into orbs that you send away from your body.

6. After 30 minutes, drain the bath and blow out the candle.

7. Perform this ritual as often as needed.

Travel Blessing Charm

Are you traveling by air, land, or sea? Drive away fear and worry with a travel blessing to encourage only positivity and safety in your travels. This spell can also be used on fellow travelers who need a protective blessing.

WHEN TO PERFORM THIS SPELL:
On a Wednesday or during a
dark moon or full moon

TIME TO ALLOT FOR THE SPELL:
15 minutes

WHERE TO PERFORM THE SPELL:
Altar or outdoors

INGREDIENTS/TOOLS:
Lighter or matches
Charcoal disc
Fire-safe plate
Small bowl
1 teaspoon dried comfrey
1 teaspoon dried rosemary
1 teaspoon dried mint
Crystal that relates to your
trip (e.g., aquamarine for
sea travel or emerald for
land travel)

1. Cleanse your altar or outdoor space.

2. Light a charcoal disc on a fire-safe plate. Allow it to heat for 5 to 10 minutes or until it glows red.

3. In a small bowl, mix the comfrey, rosemary, and mint.

4. Sprinkle a pinch of the incense mixture on the charcoal disc.

5. Pass your crystal through the incense smoke. Focus your intentions on blessing and protecting the one who carries the crystal.

Forgiving Shower Steamers

Forgiving others isn't easy—it takes courage, but doing it makes you stronger. The shower steamers in this spell are infused with calming scents and essential oils that promote courage. Use these steamers on their own or with the Cleansing Shower to Forgive spell (page 184).

WHEN TO PERFORM THIS SPELL:
On a Sunday, Wednesday, or during a new moon

TIME TO ALLOT FOR THE SPELL:
20 minutes, plus 24 to 48 hours drying time

WHERE TO PERFORM THE SPELL:
Kitchen

INGREDIENTS/TOOLS:
Medium mixing bowl and spoon
1 cup baking soda
½ cup sea salt
Spray bottle filled with water
10 drops lavender essential oil
10 drops peppermint essential oil
10 drops rosemary essential oil
Silicone molds or muffin tin

1. Cleanse your kitchen space.

2. In a bowl, combine the baking soda and salt.

3. Spray water on the baking soda and salt mixture and stir until you get a damp sand–like consistency. Add more water if necessary.

4. Stir in lavender, peppermint, and rosemary essential oils while focusing on your intentions.

5. Firmly pack the mixture into silicone molds or a muffin tin. Leave out to dry for 24 to 48 hours.

6. Remove the dry shower steamer tablets from the mold or tin and store in a sealed container.

Cleansing Shower to Forgive

Forgiveness begins from within. Only you can decide when you're ready to let go and move on. With this cleansing spell, you'll be a step closer to moving forward. Please note that this spell uses running water and therefore can only be performed in a shower.

WHEN TO PERFORM THIS SPELL:
On a Sunday, Wednesday, or
  during a new moon

TIME TO ALLOT FOR THE SPELL:
20 minutes

WHERE TO PERFORM THE SPELL:
Bathroom

INGREDIENTS/TOOLS:
Forgiving Shower Steamers
  (page 183)
Shower

1. Cleanse your bathroom.

2. Place a forgiving steamer in the corner of your shower. Begin your shower as normal.

3. When you smell the aromas from the steamer, think about the person who did you wrong and all the feelings associated with them and what they did.

4. As you wash yourself, say,
   "I wash away the pain,
   and send it down the drain;
   I forgive with heart and mind,
   and banish hurt behind."

Shielding Mist

This shielding mist is a cleansing and protective spray that makes use of the purifying power of water and the protective properties of essential oils. Carry this spray with you for when you need shielding on the go.

WHEN TO PERFORM THIS SPELL:
On a Saturday, or during a dark moon

TIME TO ALLOT FOR THE SPELL:
20 minutes

WHERE TO PERFORM THE SPELL:
Altar or kitchen

INGREDIENTS/TOOLS:
½ cup distilled water or boiled tap water cooled to room temperature
6-ounce amber glass spray bottle
4 drops lavender essential oil
4 drops sage essential oil
4 drops cedar essential oil

1. Cleanse and prepare your area.

2. Pour the water into a glass spray bottle and add the lavender, sage, and cedar essential oils. Close and shake to combine. As you shake, infuse it with your intentions.

3. Hold the bottle between your hands and envision your energy wrapping around it, becoming a part of the liquid.

4. Shake before each use.

Psychic Protection Shield

Need a shield in a pinch? Use this simple psychic protection shield to guard against negative energy or anything bad that comes your way. This shield can be useful to avoid getting caught up in other people's emotions and preserving your energy.

WHEN TO PERFORM THIS SPELL:
Anytime

TIME TO ALLOT FOR THE SPELL:
10 minutes

WHERE TO PERFORM THE SPELL:
Altar to begin, then anywhere

INGREDIENTS/TOOLS:
Shielding Mist (page 185; optional)
Smoky quartz crystal (optional)

1. Cleanse your altar and your surrounding area. If you're on the go, you may want to spray a patch of shielding mist first.

2. Get in a comfortable position and concentrate on your breathing. For added energy, hold a smoky quartz crystal in your dominant hand.

3. Focus on your energy within. Once you can visualize it, try to expand it so that it contains your body and surrounds you. It should expand to about an inch around you. Think of this shield like a bubble.

4. Use your shield against any outside energy or force that attempts to come toward you.

5. Repeat these steps as needed.

Warrior Witch Anointing Oil

Power your inner warrior with this spelled oil. Use this blend to anoint yourself or your tools. This oil will provide a basic defense against accidents, attacks, or negativity. If applying to your skin, remember to do a patch test.

WHEN TO PERFORM THIS SPELL:
On a Thursday or during a waxing moon

TIME TO ALLOT FOR THE SPELL:
15 minutes

WHERE TO PERFORM THE SPELL:
Altar

INGREDIENTS/TOOLS:
2 tablespoons carrier oil, such as almond or jojoba oil
Small amber roller bottle or dropper bottle
2 drops cedar essential oil
2 drops geranium essential oil
2 drops rosemary essential oil

1. Cleanse your altar.

2. Pour the carrier oil into an amber roller bottle.

3. Add the cedar, geranium, and rosemary essential oils one at a time and say,

   "I shield and protect with this oil blend
   and guard against those who wish to offend."

4. Hold the bottle in your hands and envision energy wrapping around it. Charge it with your intentions.

5. Your oil is now spelled and ready to use. Anoint your pressure points, tools, candles, or objects.

Crystal Grid for Protection

Amplify your power with the help of a grid that incorporates protective stones like obsidian and hematite. Other acceptable options for this grid include black tourmaline, jet, smoky quartz, fluorite, and blue cyanite.

WHEN TO PERFORM THIS SPELL:
On a Saturday or during a
 dark moon

TIME TO ALLOT FOR THE SPELL:
30 minutes

WHERE TO PERFORM THE SPELL:
Altar or outdoors

INGREDIENTS/TOOLS:
Pen and paper
4 obsidian stones
3 hematite stones
Wand or athame

1. Cleanse your altar or outdoor space.

2. With pen and paper, create a grid shape that feels right to you. For protection crystal grids, try a hexagon. Don't place the stones in your grid formation just yet—you'll do that in step 4.

3. Hold the stones in your hands and visualize your energy and intentions mixing with them. Speak an affirmation of your choice, such as *"I charge these crystals to protect and shelter me."*

4. Use the stones to re-create the grid you designed in step 2. Start with one obsidian in the center and work outward.

5. Use your wand or athame to activate your grid. Direct your energy to link the crystals together. Say, *"I link this grid to protect and shelter me."*

6. Sit back, close your eyes, and meditate for 10 minutes on your intentions.

7. Leave your grid in place for as long as you want it to be active. Every few days, link each crystal again and say your intentions out loud.

Strengthening Your Shield

Creating a psychic shield takes effort, time, and power. This shield is based on the Psychic Protection Shield spell (page 186), with some variation. If you're new to spellcasting or are struggling to harness your energy, it's especially important to use a Protection Amulet (page 178) and Shielding Mist (page 185).

WHEN TO PERFORM THIS SPELL:
Anytime

TIME TO ALLOT FOR THE SPELL:
15 minutes

WHERE TO PERFORM THE SPELL:
Anywhere

INGREDIENTS/TOOLS:
Shielding Mist (page 185; optional)
Protection Amulet (page 178) or a crystal

1. Cleanse your surrounding area.

2. If you'd like, use Shielding Mist to lay the groundwork for your shield.

3. Purify the protection amulet or crystal so you can draw energy from it.

4. Close your eyes, focus on your breath, and engage your psychic protection shield.

5. Once it's secure, expand your shield to surround you at an arm's length away from you. Practice holding for at least 1 minute.

6. Practice steps 4 and 5 until you can reliably hold the shield for an entire minute.

7. When you're ready, push the shield past your arm's length and continue expanding to fill the entire room. As your shield expands, it banishes or drives out negative entities or unwanted energy from the space you're in.

8. Repeat as needed. Remember that practice makes perfect!

forgiveness Tarot Ritual

You can use divination to reveal the path to forgiveness. This spell is an easy tarot ritual that you can adapt to fit any situation. It focuses on what you need to overcome in order to begin your journey to forgiveness.

WHEN TO PERFORM THIS SPELL:
On a Sunday, Monday, or during a dark moon or full moon

TIME TO ALLOT FOR THE SPELL:
30 minutes

WHERE TO PERFORM THE SPELL:
Altar

INGREDIENTS/TOOLS:
Lighter or matches
White votive or tea light candle
Wand or athame
Tarot deck
Pen and paper

1. Cleanse your altar.

2. Light the candle and set your intentions.

3. You'll be taking a journey, so take extra time to create a circle of protection to protect your mind while you meditate. To do this, create a circle with your wand or athame and envision white light enforcing the barrier.

4. Ask yourself three questions: What do I need to overcome in order to begin my journey to forgiveness? How can I overcome these barriers? What is the outcome of my situation?

5. Now, sit down and overhand shuffle your tarot deck until you feel compelled to stop.

6. Lay the deck on your altar and fan out the cards.

7. Close your eyes and allow yourself to tap into your intuition.

8. Pick three cards and flip them one by one.

9. The first card is the answer to your first question, the second card is the answer to the next question, and the third card is the answer to the last question.

10. With your pen and paper, take notes on what messages you see in each card as it relates to the corresponding question.

11. When you are finished reflecting, put away your tarot cards, extinguish your candle, and close your circle.

Car Protection and Blessing

Cast this spell before getting behind the wheel. It instills safety, protection, focus, and awareness in you while you drive. This spell can be altered to protect any mode of transportation—just adjust the affirmation in step 7 and place the charm bag in your pocket or bag instead of your car.

WHEN TO PERFORM THIS SPELL:
During a new moon

TIME TO ALLOT FOR THE SPELL:
25 minutes

WHERE TO PERFORM THE SPELL:
Altar and your car

INGREDIENTS/TOOLS:
Lighter or matches
Black votive candle
10-inch square of black cloth
2 teaspoons dried mugwort
2 teaspoons dried juniper
2 teaspoons dried black salt
2 teaspoons dried
     cayenne pepper
2 teaspoons cinnamon
Turquoise stone or smoky
     quartz crystal
Pen and small piece of paper
Protection Sigil (page 179)
String

1. Cleanse your altar.

2. Light the candle and visualize your intentions.

3. Lay out the cloth and place the mugwort, juniper, black salt, cayenne pepper, and cinnamon on it. Say, *"Herbs of protection, lend your blessing."*

4. Hold the turquoise in your hand and connect with its energy. Add it to the cloth and say, *"Stone of safety, impart your properties."*

5. Draw your protection sigil on a small sheet of paper. Add the paper to the cloth and say, *"Sigil of defense, offer your shield."*

6. Pull up the sides of the cloth and tie it tightly with the string to seal it. Envision its protective energy being activated.

7. Place the charm bag in your car, under your seat, or in your glovebox. Visualize its energy surrounding the car in a white light. Say, *"Charm of protection, imbue your energy, and bless this car and all its parts."*

8. Recharge the charm bag every month.

Protection Spell Bottle

This spell bottle is long-lasting and is fueled by your intentions to guard against malevolent entities or criminal and immoral actions. To perform this spell, you'll use protection spices.

WHEN TO PERFORM THIS SPELL:
On a Tuesday or during a
new moon

TIME TO ALLOT FOR THE SPELL:
30 minutes, plus 3 to 4 hours
burn time

WHERE TO PERFORM THE SPELL:
Altar

INGREDIENTS/TOOLS:
1 tablespoon black pepper
1 tablespoon cumin
1 tablespoon sea salt or
black salt
1 tablespoon cinnamon
Small or medium glass jar
with a lid
Black pen and paper
Protection Sigil (page 179)
3 pieces of iron (e.g., iron nails
or hematite stones)
4-inch brown or black chime
candle or mini taper candle
Lighter or matches

1. Cleanse your altar.

2. Add the black pepper, cumin, salt, and cinnamon to the jar one at a time, focusing on your intentions.

3. On a sheet of paper, draw your protection sigil. Fold it and place it in your jar.

4. Add the iron pieces to the jar and close the lid.

5. Light the candle and hold it horizontally, allowing some of the wax to drip onto the lid of the jar. Let wax drip onto the lid until there is enough to stand the candle upright. Stick the candle in the wax on the lid, still lit, and hold it steady in place. Allow the wax to dry around the candle so it can stand on its own. Allow the candle to burn out, sealing your intentions into the spell bottle.

6. Place your protection spell bottle near the front of your house.

Warding Wall Hanging

Use this wall hanging to defend your home against negativity and malevolent forces. This spell also makes use of bells, knot magic, and iron, the element of earth. Hang it in your room, your office, or in the center of your home.

WHEN TO PERFORM THIS SPELL:
On a Saturday or during a
  waxing moon or new moon

TIME TO ALLOT FOR THE SPELL:
30 minutes

WHERE TO PERFORM THE SPELL:
Altar

INGREDIENTS/TOOLS:
Spool or skein of brown or
  black string or yarn
Scissors
4 (6-inch) foraged sticks
6 bell charms
6 pieces of iron (i.e., nails, nuts,
  bolts, or small cutlery)

1. Cleanse your altar.

2. Purify your ingredients.

3. Cut at least 30 (12-inch) pieces of string and set them aside.

4. Use 4 wood sticks to create a diamond shape with overlapping corners.

5. Tie the corners of the wood diamond with more string.

6. Use the string you set aside to tie cow hitch knots all along the bottom half of the diamond—as many as you can fit.

7. Tie bells and pieces of iron in different places along the hanging strings, using your intuition.

8. Hang the wall hanging up with string.

9. Your wall hanging is ready to ward off negativity and malevolent forces. It will chime when unwanted energy comes near.

CHAPTER
9

WELL-BEING, SUCCESS
&
ABUNDANCE

Well-being, success, and abundance spells can help you begin to manifest the life you want for yourself. These spells won't do all the work for you—they take a lot of energy, practice, patience, and dedication to succeed. When you begin using these spells, start simple—use your realistic personal goals to set your intentions. In this section, you'll find spells focusing on positivity, good fortune, self-care, and happiness.

Clarity Tea Spell

Use this clarity tea spell to get a clearer picture of exactly what you want to achieve. This spell can help you make sense of stressful situations, which will in turn help you relax and open up your mind.

WHEN TO PERFORM THIS SPELL:
On a Saturday, Sunday, or during a new moon

TIME TO ALLOT FOR THE SPELL:
15 minutes

WHERE TO PERFORM THE SPELL:
Kitchen

INGREDIENTS/TOOLS:
Small pot
1 cup water
½ teaspoon dried mugwort
½ teaspoon dried valerian
½ teaspoon dried chamomile
½ teaspoon cinnamon
½ teaspoon dried lavender
Muslin cloth or strainer
Cup for drinking

1. Cleanse your kitchen area.

2. In a small pot, boil the water as you set your intentions.

3. Remove the pot from the heat.

4. Add the mugwort, valerian, chamomile, cinnamon, and lavender to the pot and let the herbs steep for 10 minutes while you meditate on your intentions.

5. Strain the tea into a cup, move your hand in a clockwise direction above the cup, and say,
   "Help me see
   what is meant for me."

6. Feel the energy fusing with your tea. Drink and enjoy.

Well-Being Mirror Spell

We are often told to focus on our well-being, but it's not always easy to know where to start. This mirror spell is a good first step to finding balance, which will help you feel happy, healthy, socially connected, and purposeful. This spell uses the power of a candle, mirror, and meditation.

WHEN TO PERFORM THIS SPELL:
During a new moon

TIME TO ALLOT FOR THE SPELL:
20 minutes

WHERE TO PERFORM THE SPELL:
Altar

INGREDIENTS/TOOLS:
Compact mirror
Lighter or matches
White votive candle
Pen and paper (optional)

1. Cleanse your altar.

2. Purify the compact mirror.

3. Open the compact and set it on your altar.

4. Light the candle, place it on the mirror and say,
   *"Burning candle illuminate
   well-being I can create."*

5. As the mirror reflects the candle's light, meditate for 15 minutes on your intentions and overall well-being. Search for balance, purpose, connections, and things that will make you happy and healthy.

6. Allow messages or visions to come through that will support you in focusing on your well-being. Write them down if you wish.

7. Extinguish your candle and repeat as necessary.

Positivity Incense

Generate your own positivity with this blend of charged incense. Burn it whenever you need an emotional, mental, or spiritual boost. Positivity incense also works well in any spellwork related to manifesting or attracting success, abundance, or well-being.

WHEN TO PERFORM THIS SPELL:
On a Friday or during a
   waxing moon

TIME TO ALLOT FOR THE SPELL:
10 minutes

WHERE TO PERFORM THE SPELL:
Altar or kitchen

INGREDIENTS/TOOLS:
2- to 3-ounce glass jar with a lid
1 tablespoon dried mint
1 tablespoon dried chamomile
1 tablespoon dried thyme
1 tablespoon dried sage
1 tablespoon dried lavender

1. Cleanse your altar or kitchen space.

2. Add the mint, chamomile, thyme, sage, and lavender one at a time to the jar. Focus on letting positivity infuse the mixture and say,

   "May this mix bring positivity
   and balance to my life,
   May this mix ward against negativity,
   And banish any strife."

3. Seal the jar and give it a good shake.

4. Burn the incense in an open fire or on a charcoal disc on a heat-proof dish.

Good Fortune Charm

Craft this good fortune charm to boost your luck. This charm uses Fehu, the rune of fortune, luck, beginnings, and wealth. It is made with a carved piece of wood that you can carry with you to improve your circumstances.

WHEN TO PERFORM THIS SPELL:
On a Thursday or during a waxing moon

TIME TO ALLOT FOR THE SPELL:
15 minutes

WHERE TO PERFORM THE SPELL:
Altar or any workspace

INGREDIENTS/TOOLS:
2- to 3-inch-round foraged piece of wood
180- to 220-grit sandpaper
Knife or permanent marker

1. Cleanse your altar or workspace.

2. Begin sanding your piece of wood. Buff away any rough or jagged edges.

3. With a knife or a permanent marker, mark the rune symbol for Fehu. As you inscribe, say, *"Fehu, rune of good fortune, support me in my endeavors and bring me luck and new beginnings."*

4. Carry your good fortune charm or keep it somewhere safe for when you need it most.

Abundance Balm

An abundance balm can boost your energy to attract abundance. It will encourage joy and bring forth strength of mind, body, and soul. This balm incorporates herbs and vitamin E oil. You can also apply it to soothe dry skin.

WHEN TO PERFORM THIS SPELL:
On a Thursday or during a full moon or new moon

TIME TO ALLOT FOR THE SPELL:
25 minutes

WHERE TO PERFORM THE SPELL:
Kitchen

INGREDIENTS/TOOLS:
¼ cup white beeswax pastilles
⅓ cup virgin coconut oil
Medium microwave-safe bowl
⅓ cup almond oil
½ tablespoon vitamin E oil
3 (3-ounce) metal tins or jars

1. Cleanse your kitchen space.

2. Place the beeswax and coconut oil in a microwave-safe bowl and microwave at 30-second intervals.

3. Repeat, stirring each time, until the beeswax is completely melted. Do not allow the mixture to boil.

4. Stir in the almond and vitamin E oils and focus on your intentions to attract abundance.

5. As you stir, say,
   "Abundance, come to me."

6. When your mixture is combined, pour it into your tins or jars and allow it to set.

Self-Esteem Talisman

The worse you feel, the less motivated you are, and vice versa. Use this self-esteem talisman to reclaim your sense of worth and overcome the vicious cycle of self-doubt. Wear it whenever you need a little help believing in yourself.

WHEN TO PERFORM THIS SPELL:
On a Monday, Wednesday, Friday, or during a waxing moon

TIME TO ALLOT FOR THE SPELL:
15 minutes

WHERE TO PERFORM THE SPELL:
Altar

INGREDIENTS/TOOLS:
Positivity Incense (page 202)
Charcoal disc
Heat-proof dish
Lighter or matches
Piece of jewelry or crystal or stone pendant

1. Cleanse your altar.

2. Place the incense on the charcoal disc on a heat-proof dish. Light the incense, close your eyes, and say,
   "I release my low self-esteem and doubts into the smoke."

3. Next, meditate for 5 minutes on your intentions.

4. Open your eyes and pass the jewelry or pendant through the smoke of the incense. This will purify, cleanse, and consecrate it for use.

5. Pass it through the smoke 3 times and say,
   "With each pass, I cleanse, radiate, and shine."

6. Your talisman is now ready to be worn or carried. Recharge every few months.

Body Comfort Spell

Your body is as sacred as any other tool you use in witchcraft, so it's important to nurture and honor it and the many things it does for you. Use this spell to embrace yourself, your body, and all the things that make you who you are.

WHEN TO PERFORM THIS SPELL:
On a Monday or during a
   new moon

TIME TO ALLOT FOR THE SPELL:
15 minutes

WHERE TO PERFORM THE SPELL:
Bathroom

INGREDIENTS/TOOLS:
Mirror
Large plate
White or pink pillar candle
2 tablespoons carrier oil, such
   as olive oil or almond oil
1 tablespoon dried lavender
Fire-safe plate
Lighter or matches

1. Cleanse your bathroom.

2. Situate yourself in front of a mirror.

3. Over a large plate, coat the candle in carrier oil. Don't get any oil on the wick.

4. Sprinkle dried lavender all over the candle until coated. Focus on your intentions.

5. Place the anointed candle on a fire-safe plate in front of you and light it.

6. Stare at your reflection and say,
   "I am perfect, I am whole,
   I love myself in mind, body, and soul."

7. Repeat this spell as needed.

Inner Ambition Scrying

Activate and harness your inner ambition with the help of fire. Fire scrying is a form of divination that uses a flame to reveal messages and visions. The candle's dancing flame can show order and chaos, action, and rebirth. Fire scrying will help you get a clearer picture of your ambitions and dreams.

WHEN TO PERFORM THIS SPELL:
On a Tuesday, Sunday, or during a new moon or waxing moon

TIME TO ALLOT FOR THE SPELL:
15 minutes

WHERE TO PERFORM THE SPELL:
Altar

INGREDIENTS/TOOLS:
5 purple or white tea light candles
Lighter or matches
Purple or white votive or pillar candle
Pen and paper

1. Cleanse your altar.

2. Place the tea light candles at the points of an invisible pentagram on your altar. Light them.

3. Place the votive candle in the center of the invisible pentagram. (You'll light this candle in step 5.)

4. Close your eyes and meditate for 5 minutes on your intention.

5. When you are ready, light the center candle.

6. Concentrate on the flame. Think about your ambitions and dreams.

7. Allow the candle to reveal messages and visions, and take notes if you'd like.

Success Sigil

Attract success into your life with a success sigil. Crafting a sigil allows you to make a symbolic representation of your intentions. Sigils are a way for you to draw from within yourself to create something magical that is uniquely yours.

WHEN TO PERFORM THIS SPELL:
On a Sunday or during a
  waxing moon

INGREDIENTS/TOOLS:
Pen with orange ink
2 sheets of paper

TIME TO ALLOT FOR THE SPELL:
15 minutes

WHERE TO PERFORM THE SPELL:
Altar and outdoors

1. Cleanse your altar.

2. Craft a sentence with an affirmation of your choosing, such as "I am confident, powerful, and successful."

3. Shorten the affirmation by removing any repeated letters and vowels. For the affirmation above, you'll be left with "mcnfdtpwrls."

4. Deconstruct the remaining letters into basic strokes, like curves, dots, dashes, and lines. Draw these strokes below the abbreviated affirmation on the same paper.

5. Still on the same sheet of paper, combine the strokes to form the outline of a single shape. This could be a square, a heart, a cross, or a triangle. Place any remaining circles, arcs, and dashes along the lines or around the shape. This shape will be your success sigil.

6. Redraw your success sigil, now coded with your intentions, on the second sheet of paper. Carry it with you.

Good Luck Spell

With this spell, you can attract more luck into your life simply by offering up a penny to the world. Leaving a penny for a stranger is a great way to improve not only your luck but also your karma.

WHEN TO PERFORM THIS SPELL:
Anytime

TIME TO ALLOT FOR THE SPELL:
10 minutes

WHERE TO PERFORM THE SPELL:
Outdoors

INGREDIENTS/TOOLS:
Penny
Clear quartz crystal (optional)

1. Focus on your breathing and center yourself. If you need a boost of energy, draw from a clear quartz crystal.

2. Take the penny in your hand and imbue it with your intentions.

3. Close your eyes and say,
   "I send this penny into the world.
   Little penny bring to me
   luck and fortune times three.
   With this offering I share
   good karma to the unaware."

4. Place your penny heads-up where no one can see you and allow good fortune to find you.

Abundance Mint Tea

Invite abundance into your life with this simple-to-make but powerful tea. Mint is known for its associations with abundance, prosperity, healing, luck, and strength. This infusion can be ingested or used in the Abundance Root Spell (page 211).

WHEN TO PERFORM THIS SPELL:
During a waxing moon

TIME TO ALLOT FOR THE SPELL:
15 minutes

WHERE TO PERFORM THE SPELL:
Kitchen

INGREDIENTS/TOOLS:
Medium pot
1 quart (4 cups) water
½ cup fresh mint or ¼ cup dried mint
Muslin cloth or strainer
Cup for drinking or bottle

1. Cleanse your kitchen.

2. In a medium pot, boil the water to remove impurities.

3. Remove the pot from the heat.

4. Sprinkle in the mint and say,
   "With this herb I instill
   abundance and goodwill."

5. Meditate on your intentions for 10 minutes while the tea brews and cools.

6. Strain the tea into a cup and drink it or strain it into a bottle and pour it around your property. Alternatively, use it in the Abundance Root Spell (page 211).

Abundance Root Spell

This spell is designed to connect you with the energy of fruit-bearing trees to celebrate their abundance and draw from their energy. To amplify the spell, prepare a batch of Abundance Mint Tea (page 210).

WHEN TO PERFORM THIS SPELL:
During a waxing moon

TIME TO ALLOT FOR THE SPELL:
30 minutes, plus travel time to a fruit-bearing tree

WHERE TO PERFORM THE SPELL:
Outdoors

INGREDIENTS/TOOLS:
Fruit-bearing tree
Abundance Mint Tea (page 210) or ¼ cup dried mint

1. Find a fruit-bearing tree in your yard or in a nearby area that's safe and protected.

2. Cleanse the surrounding area by tapping into your energy and pushing it outward.

3. Place your hand on the tree and say,
   "Fruit-bearing tree, I bring to thee
   an enchanted gift, to raise and uplift."

4. Walk around the base of the tree and sprinkle mint or pour Abundance Mint Tea on the tree's roots. Say,
   "Share with me abundance times three."

5. Close your eyes and envision your connection to the tree.

Well-Being Anointing Oil

In this spell, you'll blend, charge, and bless this magical anointing oil. Use this oil on objects, in well-being spells, or on your pulse points as a way to amplify your intentions to attract positivity into your life. If applying to your skin, remember to do a patch test.

WHEN TO PERFORM THIS SPELL:
During a new or full moon

TIME TO ALLOT FOR THE SPELL:
20 minutes

WHERE TO PERFORM THE SPELL:
Altar or kitchen

INGREDIENTS/TOOLS:
Small amber roller bottle or dropper bottle
1 tablespoon carrier oil, such as jojoba or almond oil
2 drops patchouli essential oil
2 drops lavender essential oil
2 drops ylang-ylang essential oil
1 teaspoon dried chamomile

1. Cleanse your altar.

2. Add the carrier oil to an amber roller bottle.

3. Next, add in the patchouli, lavender, and ylang-ylang essential oils while focusing on your intentions.

4. Add the chamomile to fill any empty space.

5. Hold the bottle in your hands and envision energy wrapping around it. Charge it with your intentions. Say,
"With this oil I blend and bless,
well-being and feelings of gratefulness."

6. Wear it whenever you need to live in the moment and attract positivity.

Weaving Success Spell

Weave success into your life with the help of knot magic and the success rune, Sowilo. Using Sowilo in your spells can help you find guidance, master goal setting, and achieve wholeness. With this spell, you will weave together your intentions to create positive change in your life.

WHEN TO PERFORM THIS SPELL:
On a Sunday or during a
full moon

TIME TO ALLOT FOR THE SPELL:
30 minutes

WHERE TO PERFORM THE SPELL:
Altar

INGREDIENTS/TOOLS:
Knife
Orange, gold, or silver
pillar candle
Lighter or matches
3 (18-inch) pieces orange
string or yarn

1. Cleanse your altar.

2. Use a knife to carve the rune Sowilo into your candle.

3. Light the candle, set your intentions, and raise your energy.

4. Tie the three strings together at one end with a simple overhand knot. As you do this, think about attracting success in all areas of your life.

CONTINUED

5. Begin braiding the three strings and say,

   "String of goals, weave together,
   string of wholeness, connect,
   string of accomplishment, entwine.
   braid of success, interlace."

6. Knot the end of the braid. Meditate for 10 minutes and focus on what you've created, allowing yourself to feel its power.

7. When finished meditating, extinguish the candle.

8. Hang the braid wherever you need to attract more success in your life.

Success Offering Spell

This offering spell uses the energy of the noon sun and the earth's soil. The offering uses success-attracting ingredients like a cinnamon stick, fresh ginger, lemon balm, bergamot, and your Success Sigil (page 208).

WHEN TO PERFORM THIS SPELL:
At noon on the day of a new
  moon or waxing moon

TIME TO ALLOT FOR THE SPELL:
25 minutes

WHERE TO PERFORM THE SPELL:
Altar and outside

INGREDIENTS/TOOLS:
Light or matches
Orange votive candle
Pen with orange ink
Success Sigil (page 208)
Sheet of paper
1 cinnamon stick
4-inch piece of fresh
  ginger root
Sprig of fresh lemon balm
Orange string or yarn
3 drops bergamot essential oil

1. Cleanse your altar.

2. Light an orange candle for attracting success.

3. Draw your success sigil on a sheet of paper with an orange pen. This will house your offering.

4. On top of the paper, lay a cinnamon stick, ginger root, and sprig of lemon balm.

5. Focus on your intentions and fold up your paper offering. Tie a knot around it with orange string, creating a bundle.

6. Add the bergamot essential oil to the knot.

7. Meditate for 5 minutes on your intentions.

8. Extinguish the candle.

CONTINUED

9. Go outside and find a north-facing view to bury the bundle you made in step 5.

10. Dig a shallow hole with your hands and place the bundle inside. Say,
"Under the sun's mighty glow,
I gift this offering to the earth
in exchange for the success you bestow."

11. Fill the hole, place your hand on the earth, and meditate for 5 minutes.

12. Feel the energy of the sun and earth combining to bring you success.

13. Thank the sun and earth for their energy before you leave.

Planting Happiness Spell

Happiness is often just within reach, but not quite within our grasp. Cast this spell to radiate happiness that will leave you glowing and feeling in sync with the moment. In this spell, you'll plant a tree or shrub, which will allow you to find happiness in nature.

WHEN TO PERFORM THIS SPELL:
On a Wednesday or Sunday

TIME TO ALLOT FOR THE SPELL:
45 minutes

WHERE TO PERFORM THE SPELL:
Outdoors

INGREDIENTS/TOOLS:
Shielding Mist (page 185; optional)
Shovel
Plant or tree
5 clear quartz crystals
Gardening gloves (optional)
Shovel
Water (enough to water your plant—the amount varies from plant to plant, so do your research!)
Dash salt

1. Use your intuition to choose an outdoor spot (e.g., somewhere in your garden) for your happiness plant or tree.

2. Cleanse the chosen area. If you'd like to, spray it with Shielding Mist.

3. Use the tip of the shovel to scratch out a pentagram shape in the earth that encompasses you and your plant.

4. Place the clear quartz crystals at the points of the pentagram.

5. Begin digging a hole in the soil. Wear gardening gloves if you'd like.

6. Place your plant or tree in the hole. Pack dirt up to the base of the plant to stabilize it.

CONTINUED

7. Spend 10 minutes meditating silently next to the plant, reaching out with your consciousness to connect with its energy. While meditating, say,

"Plant of happiness,
fill my life,
brighten my heart,
and lift my spirit."

8. Water your plant and sprinkle the salt as an offering in the surrounding area.

9. Care for your plant weekly, repeating your meditation and chant.

Success Rune Cookies

Bring some witchery into your baking with these success rune cookies! This recipe for spelled cookies is designed to help you raise your energy to achieve your goals. Each cookie is decorated with the success rune, Sowilo, to promote success, wholeness, and achievement.

WHEN TO PERFORM THIS SPELL:
On a Sunday or during a
  new moon

TIME TO ALLOT FOR THE SPELL:
30 minutes

WHERE TO PERFORM THE SPELL:
Kitchen

INGREDIENTS:
2¾ cups all-purpose flour
1 teaspoon baking soda
½ teaspoon baking powder
1 cup butter, at room
  temperature
1½ cups sugar
1 egg
1 teaspoon vanilla extract

1. Cleanse your kitchen.

2. Preheat the oven to 375°F.

3. In a small bowl, mix the flour, baking soda, and baking powder. Set aside.

4. In a large bowl, beat the butter and sugar until smooth. Beat in the egg and vanilla extract.

5. Fold the dry ingredients into the wet and mix until just combined into a dough.

6. Roll the dough into 3-inch balls and flatten them on a cookie sheet.

CONTINUED

7. Using a knife, draw the rune Sowilo on each cookie while focusing on your intentions.

8. Bake for 8 to 10 minutes or until golden.

9. Let the cookies sit for 2 minutes, then transfer them to a wire rack to cool.

10. Eat the cookies to connect with and internalize Sowilo's energy.

Blanket of Security Spell

In this spell, you'll enchant an ordinary blanket with comfort and security and imbue it with an encoded sigil. Keep it for yourself or give it as a gift to young ones. It's a good idea to cleanse the blanket before using it in the spell so no old or stagnant energies remain.

WHEN TO PERFORM THIS SPELL:
On a Saturday, Sunday, or during a full moon

TIME TO ALLOT FOR THE SPELL:
30 minutes

WHERE TO PERFORM THE SPELL:
Altar

INGREDIENTS/TOOLS:
Blanket
Lighter or matches
Purple candle
Permanent marker
Security sigil

1. Cleanse your altar.

2. Purify the blanket.

3. Light the candle and focus on your intentions to manifest comfort, security, and stability.

4. Hold the blanket in your arms and say,
   "Like the earth, enduring and strong,
   I bless this blanket to protect and last long.
   Like the fire, warming and light,
   I bless this blanket to comfort each night.
   Like the water, healing and pure,
   I bless this blanket to keep safe and secure.
   Like the air, swift to inspire,
   I bless this blanket to uplift and meet desire."

5. Meditate for 5 minutes on your intentions to charge the blanket.

6. Create a security sigil. Use the instructions for the Protection Sigil (page 179), replacing the word *protect* with *security*. Draw your security sigil on the label of the blanket.

Witch's Ladder for Success and Abundance

Inspire success and abundance through a life-size witch's ladder. A witch's ladder comes from folk magic and incorporates knot magic. It's best used to complement meditation and rituals relating to success and abundance.

WHEN TO PERFORM THIS SPELL:
On a Saturday, Sunday, or during a full moon

TIME TO ALLOT FOR THE SPELL:
45 minutes

WHERE TO PERFORM THE SPELL:
Altar

INGREDIENTS/TOOLS:
3 candles in orange, white, and blue
Lighter or matches
3 skeins of yarn in orange, white, and blue
Scissors
9 adornments of your choosing (e.g., beads, feathers, or mini bell charms)

1. Cleanse your altar.

2. Place the candles in a triangular configuration on the altar and light them.

3. From each skein of yarn, cut a piece that measures the length of your body.

4. Tie the three pieces of yarn together at one end with a basic overhand knot.

5. Choose 9 evenly spaced sections where you will tie your adornments as you braid the strings.

6. Begin braiding the strings. At the beginning of each new section, tie in one of your nine adornments with a knot.

7. As you make each knot, feel free to chant the traditional witch's ladder incantation:

   "By knot of one, the spell's begun.
   By knot of two, the magic comes true.
   By knot of three, so it shall be.
   By knot of four, this power is stored.
   By knot of five, my will shall drive.
   By knot of six, the spell I fix.
   By knot of seven, the future I leaven.
   By knot of eight, my will be fate.
   By knot of nine, what is done is mine."

8. When you are finished braiding, knot the end. Find a safe place to hang your witch's ladder, such as a closet in your home.

Resources

Witchology Magazine

My monthly magazine for modern witchcraft and magic. This is a valuable resource written by a team of seasoned writers who share their own paths with their readers.

Cunningham's Encyclopedia of Magical Herbs, by Scott Cunningham

This is a must for any beginner witch. It contains properties, history, and uses for over 400 herbs. Use this encyclopedia whenever you need to incorporate herbs into your spells.

The Complete Book of Incense, Oils and Brews, by Scott Cunningham

This is one of my personal favorites. After you learn the basics about how herbs, spices, and plants can be used in your practice, this book will take your craft a step further and assist you in creating custom incense blends, magical oils, potions, and other useful brews.

Cunningham's Encyclopedia of Crystal, Gem & Metal Magic, by Scott Cunningham

Working with the natural elements of the earth is a major part of any witch's practice. This book of over 100 gems and metals will help you figure out which crystal, gem, or metal will work best in your spell.

Llewellyn's Witches' Datebook

This comes out each year and helps you stay organized and keep track of the Wheel of the Year and astrological movements. Use this to keep track of the spells you cast and plan out the year ahead.

Coloring Book of Shadows, by Amy Cesari

Starting out as a new witch can be very overwhelming, but not with this book of shadows. You can color as you learn about crystals, herbs, and other natural elements. Tailor it to your own path and fill it with your first spells.

Index

Acknowledgments

My thanks go to my amazing support team who helped me write this book: My wonderful partner, Leon, thank you for your encouragement during the writing process. My adorable familiar, Nala, who sat with me every day while writing this book. My amazing sister, Sylvia, who always pushes me to be my best. The *Witchology* team, for continuing to create amazing work for the magazine in my absence while I wrote this book. Claire Yee, my wonderful editor, for weaving her magic to help the words in this book come alive.

About the Author

AMBROSIA HAWTHORN is a California-born traveling eclectic witch with indigenous roots in Yup'ik shamanism and Puerto Rican folk magic.

She is the owner of Wild Goddess Magick, a witchcraft blog, and the editor of *Witchology Magazine*. In her spare time, she navigates the stars as an astrologer and connects to the universe as a card slinger. She found her practice at the age of 13 and has been studying the craft and her lineage ever since. Ambrosia's goal is to provide material for every kind of witch, and she uses the Wheel of the Year to create and share new content about all types of magic.

NOTES

NOTES

NOTES

NOTES

NOTES

NOTES

NOTES

NOTES

NOTES